REACTION:

THE NATIONAL ENERGY PROGRAM

REACTION:
THE NATIONAL ENERGY PROGRAM

Contributors include
T.J. Courchene, K.H. Norrie,
and J.G. Stabback

Co-Edited by G.C. Watkins
and M.A. Walker

THE FRASER INSTITUTE
1981

Canadian Cataloguing in Publication Data
Main entry under title:
Reaction

ISBN 0-88975-042-4
1. Canada. National Energy Program.
2. Energy policy — Canada. I. Courchene, Thomas J., 1940- II. Norrie, K.H. (Kenneth Harold), 1946- III. Stabback, J.G. (Jack Garry) IV. Watkins, G.C. (Gordon Campbell), 1939- V. Walker, Michael, 1945- VI. Fraser Institute (Vancouver, B.C.)
HD9502.C32R4 333.79 C81-091093-4

Printed in Canada

CONTENTS

Chapter 2: Canadian Energy Policy: Financing Our Energy Future

Jack G. Stabback, *Vice President and Head*
and
Daryll G. Waddingham, *Senior Energy Advisor*

Energy and Mineral Resource Department
Global Energy Group
Royal Bank of Canada, Calgary

Chapter 3: Mr. Lalonde and the Price Mechanism: Or Never the Twain Shall Meet

G. Campbell Watkins, *President, DataMetrics Limited and Visiting Professor of Economics, University of Calgary*

Chapter 5: The National Energy Program: A Western Perspective

Kenneth H. Norrie, *Department of Economics, University of Alberta*

Chapter 6: The National Energy Program and Canadian Financial Markets

John A.G. Grant, *Director and Chief Economist*
Wood Gundy Limited, Toronto

Reaction: The National Energy Program

Preface

I. INTRODUCTION

On October 28, 1980, the Federal Government introduced its National Energy Program (NEP). The period since its release has been characterized by hostile though measured reaction from the industry and the oil producing provinces. The provisions of the program have precipitated an unprecedented retaliation on the part of the Government of Alberta in the form of a cut-back in oil deliveries to the East and provided devastating ammunition to the promoters of western separation. Meanwhile, the country's energy future lies in precarious jeopardy as the all-important development of synthetic oil supplies has ground to a halt and conventional exploration activity shifts to the U.S.

It is ironic that a program of government, ostensibly designed to "secure the nation's energy future" should have such a damaging effect on the industrial sectors and the provinces uniquely capable of achieving it. Perhaps it is this inconsistency that has led some observers to claim that the new energy program is, in fact, a political document more concerned about short-run political objectives than energy security.

The various papers by prominent Canadians in this volume provide strong and unfortunate evidence that, whatever its merits as a political stratagem, the NEP is defective as an economic policy, and, if the economic objectives addressed by the policy are to be achieved, the energy program must be revised in the light of the realities which, for whatever reason, it failed to probe. In other words, if the interests of the nation are to be served, the NEP ought to be regarded as a "first draft" of the policy that will guide Canada's energy future rather than a final, immutable statement of it.

In this spirit and with the belief that, being reasonable men, the Federal Cabinet will respond to rational argument, the Fraser Institute is publishing this critique of the energy program.

The highlights

The papers in this volume have been written in a non-technical way with the objective of involving as wide a readership as possible. And, I commend them to the reader as an excellent source of opinion on these vital issues. Because not all readers will have the time or the inclination to read all of the papers, I have provided in the following pages a brief summary of the main points. However, this summary does not cover all of the material in the volume and is no substitute for reading the various papers if a complete grasp of the critique is desired.

II. ACHIEVING OIL SECURITY

Demand factors

The keystone of the NEP is a reduction in total use of crude oil of 11.4 per cent below the 1979 level, by 1985. This reduction is to be achieved via a decrease in the demand for oil directly and indirectly through a process of substituting natural gas for crude oil. The conclusion of the various authors is that this objective is unlikely to be realized both because there will be insufficient incentive to generally economize on the use of oil, particularly in the transportation sector, and because the gasification program in the Maritimes will be unlikely to achieve the extent of crude oil replacement anticipated in the program.

The main defect in the NEP from the point of view of conservation is the fact that the price of crude oil is not escalated quickly enough to take advantage of the natural conservation effects which are induced by rising price. It has been calculated, for example, that if refiners continue to pass along crude oil price increases in the same fashion as they have done in the past, the price of refined products will decline in real terms during the first few years of the program. That is to say, the price of gasoline, for example, will rise less quickly than the general rate of inflation predicted by the government in the budget which accompanied the NEP.

The additional oil consumption induced by the less than world level of prices will amount to 108 million barrels per year by 1984 at a total cost for the economy of some $8 billion. Of this, $1.2 billion will simply be wasted in the sense that no benefit, either direct or indirect, will be gained by that amount of the additional consumption.

Supply factors

The optimistic projection of oil supply contained in the NEP is based on a surge in oil output from synthetic oil plants during the latter part of the decade and makes provision for a gradual decline in conventional oil sources. It is the opinion of the various authors that this projected oil supply pattern may, in the event, be entirely optimistic, both because of the fact that conventional oil development has been relatively discouraged and because the increased supply from synthetics may not come on stream as quickly as anticipated.

The clear focus of the supply initiatives in the budget are on the frontier oil pools and in the area of synthetics. The principal source of supply between now and the mid-1980s will have to continue to be conventional oil sources. Unfortunately, the budget provisions have placed this conventional supply in a very precarious position. The net impact of the elimination of depletion and the eight per cent tax on operating revenues, has been to render many typical exploration projects economically infeasible because they make the net anticipated value of conventional exploration negative. Even before the budget measures were announced the existing system of federal and provincial taxes had made Alberta an unattractive location for conventional oil exploration by comparison with the United States where the producers can expect to receive world oil prices for any new oil discovered.

An apparently unanticipated impact of the NEP on conventional oil sources is that it will make in-fill drilling uneconomic. In-fill drilling is critical for maintaining the flow rates from already discovered oil pools. The rate of flow from conventional sources which is assumed in the NEP, can only be achieved if in-fill drilling is used to accelerate the rate of flow from existing reservoirs. If this program of in-fill drilling is terminated by the various producers, which seems likely, the rate of flow assumed in the budget will not be realized.

A critical feature of the projected oil supplies in the budget is the development of synthetic oil plants. Several authors have raised questions about the feasibility of these projections, however, both because of delays that seem likely to be experienced and because the overall impact of the NEP has been to make the environment inhospitable for the capital that will be necessary to develop these projects. The delays which have already been experienced because of the impasse between Ottawa and Alberta, will result in a bunching of the projected synthetic plants around the mid part of the decade and several authors have raised questions about the possibility of this bunching introducing further delays because of the capacity limitations of the construction sector.

The cost of delay in the program of synthetic oil production will be quite enormous. By 1987, for example, a one year delay in the Cold Lake and Alsands projects will cost the Canadian economy some $8 billion. The overall effect of the NEP on the discovery rate of new oil will cost the economy some $2.2 billion per year by 1984.

III. THE CANADIANIZATION OBJECTIVE

A central thrust of the NEP is the Canadianization of the petroleum industry. The pursuit of this objective is seen to stem from long-standing political anxiety about the level of foreign ownership of Canadian industry in general and is shown to be consistent with the views expressed by the Prime Minister in a celebrated article which he wrote in 1958. Moreover, the Canadianization objective is shown to be only the latest in a series of activities on the part of the Federal Government to achieve the objective of more Canadian ownership in the industry.

Chapter I, in reviewing the factual basis for this Canadianization initiative, shows that the NEP document is selective in its use of data, that Statistics Canada information does not substantiate the impression given by the figures cited by the NEP and, moreover, that the extent of Canadian ownership in the industry had been dramatically increasing prior to the promulgation of the program.

While there is undoubtedly a great deal of popular support for the Canadian ownership objective, the analysis in this volume suggests that one of the costs of achieving that objective may be a considerable shortfall in the supply of oil available from domestic sources. It seems reasonable to wonder whether popular support for the Canadianization objective would be as strong if the costs in terms of oil insecurity were generally known.

IV. SHARING THE OIL REVENUES

The third major objective of the NEP is to ensure a fair distribution of the revenues from the exploitation of Canadian petroleum resources. Unfortunately, in analyzing the fairness objective, the NEP provides an entirely distorted view of the existing allocation of these shares. The principal source of this distortion is the fact that the energy program ignores the very substantial subsidy provided to consumers via the federal policy of maintaining the oil prices below the world level.

The appropriate reference point for the calculation of shares ought to be world prices since the real value of the total energy resource pie is the value that could be achieved from simply exporting all Canadian energy resources to eager customers in other countries. The calculations performed in the NEP ignore what the total actual value of the energy resource pie is and allocate shares on the basis of the existing total revenue flow. It is on this basis, and only upon this basis, that the federal share can be shown to be smaller than the provincial share.

The existing actual shares are a legacy of the decision in 1973 to maintain Canadian oil prices below the world level. At that point, the Province of Alberta agreed to less than complete compensation for the true value of its energy resources on the basis that there would be a gradual progression toward the world price and the less than complete compensation was Alberta's contribution toward the adjustment to the higher level of prices. The difference between the actual price of energy resources and the suppressed domestic price, amounted to a tax collected by Ottawa and distributed to Canadian consumers. The implicit understanding was that as world prices rose, the Canadian price would eventually overtake it and the share implicitly absorbed by Ottawa would fall. The NEP is essentially an attempt to freeze Ottawa's share of the total energy resource pie and to reallocate its use from subsidies to consumers, to the general revenue needs of the Federal Government.

The importance of this implicit subsidy to consumers cannot be over-estimated and has clear political value to Ottawa. This was made dramatically clear in the recent federal election which was fought basically on the grounds of the extent to which the incumbent Conservative government proposed to eliminate the subsidy and the extent to which the now-incumbent Liberal government promised not to eliminate it.

The shares of the total energy resource pie calculated on the appropriate basis are 56.7 per cent for the Federal Government, 19.6 per cent for the industry, and 23.7 per cent for Alberta. Of the total government revenue involved, 70.5 per cent accrues to the Federal Government and 29.5 per cent accrues to the Alberta government. The unilateral attempt by Ottawa to rigidify this sharing arrangement, will have very long-term effects on federal/provincial relations and, as is already evident, may jeopardize the future of the Federation. It is the view of several authors that the only appropriate and fair distribution of the resource revenues must acknowledge the essential ownership rights of the Province of Alberta, something which the NEP manifestly does not do.

V. THE NATIONAL ENERGY PROGRAM AND CONFEDERATION

While the NEP is obviously of great importance in determining Canada's energy future, its most profound and long-lasting effects may be on the structure of the Canadian Federation. In fact, Professor Tom Courchene, an internationally-acknowledged expert on matters of fiscal federalism, suggests that the NEP has effectively shattered the concept of Federalism as a system of "self rule, shared rule."

In his insightful analysis, Courchene concludes that the most devastating feature of the NEP is the fact that it involves unilateral action and revokes a long-standing tradition of cooperation in the evolution of fiscal arrangements. In his view, there are no longer ground rules for the Federalism game. While the NEP itself directly impacts only a narrow range of issues, it will have an effect on the overall tone of federal/provincial fiscal dealings. In Courchene's view, the medium is the message and the medium is one of unilateral action — a message which the provinces have clearly received.

Courchene also questions whether or not the NEP is constitutionally faithful in the sense that the tax provisions of the NEP effectively amount to attacks on the property of the provinces. Section 125 of the *British North America Act* explicitly prohibits the taxation of lands or property belonging to either Canada or the provinces, a fact which has already led to a provincial challenge of the propriety of the federal actions.

A particularly important provision of the NEP is the differentiation of the effect tax provisions which apply in the Canada Lands and those which will apply in provincial lands. This, in effect, encourages the provincial governments to adopt their own taxation measures applying only to provincial lands. This encourages the use of provincial tax systems for provincial development and will, in Courchene's estimation, encourage "beggar my neighbour" type policies whereby individual provincial governments use their tax systems to attempt to attract economic activity away from other provinces. In the case of Alberta, the NEP has provided encouragement and incentive for the use of the Heritage Savings Trust Fund as a device to advance the industrial interests of Alberta at the expense of other provinces.

Thus, the most important long-term consequence of the NEP may be the further decline of the common market which exists between the provinces with all of the inefficiencies that portends. In Courchene's view, the future of Confederation and federal/provincial relations looks bleak and fractious.

VI. GENERAL ECONOMIC IMPACT

The NEP will, according to the authors, depress the overall level of economic activity in the petroleum industry in the foreseeable future, both because of its direct effects and because of the uncertainty it creates about the future. The incidence of these effects will be primarily in the West but will, via the usual channels, have an increasing effect elsewhere in the country as time passes. The elimination of one of the country's only growth poles in a time of already sluggish economic performance, will have great costs in terms of higher unemployment and will jeopardize the rate of recovery of the economy as the current slump comes to an end.

The delay of the large synthetic oil projects will contribute to this economic contraction. However, in terms of the way the economy is expected to develop over the longer term, these delays have more ominous overtones. In the next two to three years the Canadian economy is expected to generate an ample flow of savings, and large-scale energy projects would have provided a timely application for these funds. Their delay will mean a pattern of excess saving in the near term and insufficient savings toward the middle of the decade when savings flows are expected to be more modest. The net consequence of delay in the major projects will probably be a more concentrated bunching of energy expenditures around 1985 with potentially severe inflationary consequences. This inflation threat will pose a further challenge for macro-economic stabilization policy to prevent a major rekindling of inflation which is, by that time, anticipated to have somewhat abated.

VII. CONCLUSIONS

The major reservations about the NEP raised by the papers in this volume suggest that if the Federal government has the true long-term interests of the nation at heart, it must seriously reconsider the various provisions of the program. Indeed, as this book goes to press, there is some indication that such reconsideration is already in progress. This sign of good faith on the part of the government is applauded and we hope that it marks the beginning of a total reconsideration of the energy program and that subsequent revisions will reflect a greater emphasis on the security of supply and less emphasis on the issues of ownership and sharing. It is also to be hoped that the intransigent attitude of the government with regard to the fiscal negotiations with the provinces will be modified and that the future of the Federation will not be placed in further jeopardy.

The Fraser Institute has an abiding concern for rational economic policy and is publishing this volume in the interests of encouraging more informed and wider public debate about the issues raised by the National Energy Program. However, the authors have conducted their work independently and the views they express may or may not conform singly or collectively with those of the members of the Fraser Institute.

January 1981 M.A. Walker

Chapter 1

The National Energy Program: An Overview of Its Impact and Objectives

MICHAEL A. WALKER
Director,
The Fraser Institute

THE AUTHOR

MICHAEL A. WALKER is Director of the Fraser Institute. Born in Newfoundland in 1945, he received his B.A. (Summa) at St. Francis Xavier University in 1966 and his Ph.D. in Economics at the University of Western Ontario in 1969. From 1969 to 1973, he worked in various research capacities at the Bank of Canada, Ottawa, and when he left in 1973 was Research Officer in charge of the Special Studies and Monetary Policy Group in the Department of Banking. Immediately prior to joining the Fraser Institute, Dr. Walker was Econometric Model Consultant to the Federal Department of Finance, Ottawa. Dr. Walker has also taught Monetary Economics and Statistics at the University of Western Ontario and Carleton University.

Dr. Walker was editor of, and a contributor to, 11 of the Fraser Institute's previous books: *Rent Control — A Popular Paradox* (1975); *The Illusion of Wage and Price Control* (1976); *How Much Tax Do You Really Pay?* (1976); *Which Way Ahead? Canada After Wage and Price Control* (1977); *Public Property? The Habitat Debate Continued* (1977, with Lawrence B. Smith); *Oil in the Seventies: Essays on Energy Policy* (1977, with G. Campbell Watkins); *Unemployment Insurance: Global Evidence of its Effects on Unemployment* (1978, with Herbert G. Grubel); *Canadian Confederation at the Crossroads: The Search for a Federal-Provincial Balance* (1979); *Tax Facts* (1979, with Sally C. Pipes); *Unions and the Public Interest* (1980); *Rent Control: Myths & Realities* (1981).

Dr. Walker is a regular economic commentator on national television and radio and, in addition, addresses university students and a large number of service and professional organizations on Canadian public policy issues.

The National Energy Program: An Overview of Its Impact and Objectives

MICHAEL A. WALKER
Director,
The Fraser Institute

I. INTRODUCTION

The National Energy Program (NEP), announced in conjunction with the federal government's budget of October 28, 1980, will be seen in the perspective provided by the passage of time as a milestone in Canadian economic history. It marks an abrupt reversal of the policy thrust, established in the last months of the former Liberal government and continued by the Conservative government, toward more reliance on private initiative as a principal driving force in the Canadian economy. It is also a harbinger of a return to a policy climate so familiar in the mid-1970s, wherein private sector undertakings were regarded with suspicion and their vilification used as the raw material for crafting political stratagems.

As the Honourable Marc Lalonde noted in the introduction to the NEP, it is difficult to over-estimate the importance of the new energy policy. It will "impinge in almost every sphere of Canadian activity, on the fortunes of every Canadian, and on the economic and social structure of the nation for years to come."[1] Mr. Lalonde goes on to note that the new policy will have "major positive implications for the Federation itself."

While there can be no doubt that the new energy policy will have widespread economic, political and social impacts, given the reaction to the new policy in the period since its promulgation, one can have serious question about the extent to which the ultimate effect of the program will be positive. As this paper and the other papers in this volume make quite clear, the new energy program is not unambiguously positive in its effects and where they are positive, the effects are likely to be less impressive than the authors of the energy policy are inclined to believe.

The first thing that strikes one in reading the document associated with the enunciation of the policy, is that it is not strictly speaking, an economic document. Nor is it, in the sense that we have historically come to expect, a neutral document with regard to the policies which it proposes. That is to say, it does not infer from a careful articulation of the facts what an appropriate policy would be. It rather presents policies or, in the words of Mr. Lalonde, "decisions," which are then justified on the basis of appeal to a selective rendition of the facts. Because of this and because of the sweeping provisions of the new program, it is appropriate to regard the new policy as a harbinger of the political, social, philosophical and economic philosophies that will pervade policy determination under the present government, rather than solely as a technical document relating to the energy sector. And, indeed, the conclusion that is suggested by a careful assessment of the program both in this paper and in the other papers in the volume, is that the NEP will be much more successful in achieving this broader objective than it will be in solving the energy problem that Canada faces.

In order to properly assess the NEP, it is first of all appropriate to consider the historical context into which it has been launched and, in particular, to consider the set of economic problems that it proposes to solve. This is the objective of the second section of the paper. The third section of the paper summarizes the objectives of the program while the fourth considers its implications for Canada's energy problem. Section five provides a discussion of the historical context of the NEP preparatory to a discussion of the Canadianization objective in section six. A brief summary and conclusion is provided in section seven.

II. THE CANADIAN ENERGY PROBLEM

Canadians use most energy

Canadians have always been heavy users of energy. In part this reflects nothing more than the climate, geography and industrial structure of the country. But, to a certain degree, it also reflects individual preferences and the economic choices that Canadians have made when faced with the relative prices of energy and other commodities. While climate, geography and industrial structure are slow to change if at all, the relative prices of commodities do exhibit marked changes over time. In the case of energy, dramatic price changes have been occurring for many decades. In the 1950s and 1960s this was largely a declining trend as both the nominal and the relative prices of energy, particularly petroleum-based energy, were declining. And, of course, this latter development encouraged very widespread use of petroleum-based energy in Canada and, indeed, in the rest of the world as well.

In 1973 the real price of energy as well as its nominal price, began to escalate dramatically as the OPEC nations took advantage of the strong world-wide demand for petroleum and the shrinking rate of discovery of new sources. Those rapid price increases may have been expected to have an effect on the demand for petroleum in the same way that the dramatically declining prices boosted petroleum consumption in the post-war decades. However, Canadian energy policy, in the post-1973 period, has been to insulate Canadian oil consumption from the effect of rising prices. Thus, unlike most other industrial nations, Canada has not been effective in reducing the consumption of petroleum products. Currently, Canadians have the dubious distinction of being the highest per capita consumers of energy in the world.[2] Needless to say, this poses certain problems and certain opportunities for current policy development.

Not enough oil

While Canadians are the most intensive energy users of any country in the world, we are also fortunate in having one of the most expansive supplies relative to our population size. And as a consequence of this relative abundance of supply, Canada is not in the position of having an energy deficit in total terms. The difficulty we do have is a mismatch between the pattern of energy demands and the pattern of Canadian energy supplies. In particular, while Canada is a net exporter of energy in total, we nevertheless have a shortfall of liquid hydrocarbon energy sources. The consequence of this shortfall has been a steady increase in the extent to which Canada relies on imported crude oil to satisfy the demand for it. Fortunately, Canada is still a net exporter of energy, primarily on the basis of large exports of natural gas. However, the net energy trade balance has shrunk dramatically, decreasing from

1,647 trillion Btu's in 1973 to only 360 trillion Btu's in 1978. This decline primarily reflects the increased imports of crude oil.

A mounting energy deficit

In 1978 net imports of crude oil amounted to about 200,000 barrels per day. On the basis of developments which were anticipated to occur before the promulgation of the NEP, forecasts were that net imports of oil would rise steadily through the 1980s and by the mid point of the decade have tripled from their 1978 level. Projecting the various figures in Table I forward suggests that Canada will, in fact, be a net energy importer by the mid-1980s principally on the basis of the projected increase in the importation of oil. There is, of course, some possibility that exports of natural gas will mitigate the effects of increasing crude oil imports but the current conditions in the U.S. gas market suggest that is a rescue upon which we cannot comfortably depend.

TABLE I
CANADA'S NET EXPORTS OF PRIMARY ENERGY
(trillion Btu's)

	Coal	Crude Oil*	Natural Gas	Hydro & Nuclear	Total
1970	-384	299	768	8	689
1971	-259	258	897	13	909
1972	-226	468	993	30	1,266
1973	-143	729	1,012	48	1,647
1974	-74	323	946	45	1,240
1975	-112	-118	937	25	733
1976	-90	-357	950	32	534
1977	-101	-530	1,000	54	421
1978	-27	-594	881	66	328

*Including LPG's
Figures may not add due to rounding.
Source: Statistics Canada, Cat. No. 57-003 and 57-207.

The energy problem in brief

In sum, Canada's short-run energy problem is a 20 per cent shortfall of liquid petroleum supplies relative to current consumption. Best estimates are that this shortfall will grow to about 35 per cent of total consumption requirements in the mid-1980s and, as a consequence, we will have increasingly to rely on imports of foreign oil supplies to satisfy domestic demand. Both because of the impact of these imports on our balance of trade, and because of the uncertainty attaching to the continuance of supply from traditional sources, it is evident that the energy problem is, in effect, the problem of encouraging conservation, substitution to alternative energy sources, and the development of more reliable (even if higher cost) domestic supplies. Since, as we have indicated, Canada is the highest per capita user of energy in the world, it will be very difficult to achieve meaningful reductions in the demand for petroleum products in the short run, unless very effective and extensive conservation measures are undertaken. These difficulties in prospect suggest that the primary emphasis of the solution to the energy problem will have to come on the side of increasing the supplies of energy resources which can be substituted for liquid hydrocarbons and the encouragement of alternative sources of petroleum supply.

Quite apart from the overall national difficulty of a prospective, large oil deficit with the rest of the world, Canada also has internal problems related to the use of petroleum. These problems, which are made quite clear in Table II, relate to the fact that some areas of the country, particularly the Maritimes, are much more intensive users of crude oil than is typical for the nation as a whole. As can be seen in Table II, the percentage of total energy supplied by crude petroleum ranges from a low of 34 per cent in Alberta to a high of 78 per cent in the Atlantic Region. The overall national average is about 45 per cent. One obvious reason for the relatively high consumption of energy in the Maritime Provinces is, of course, the fact that they do not as yet have access to natural gas.

TABLE II
REGIONAL GROSS DOMESTIC ENERGY CONSUMPTION AND PER CENT DISTRIBUTION BY FUEL SOURCE, 1978

	Atlantic	Quebec	Ontario	Manitoba	Saskatchewan	Alberta	B.C.	Canada*
			(trillion Btu's)					
Total Consumption	680	2267	3061	341	364	932	922	8592
			Fuel Source in Per Cent					
Coal	6	1	15	3	19	16	1	9
Crude Oil & LPG's	78	47	41	38	41	34	41	45
Natural Gas	0	4	22	22	33	48	17	18
Hydro & Nuclear	15	48	22	37	7	2	41	28

*Includes Yukon and Northwest Territories.
Source: Statistics Canada Cat. No. 57-003.

III. THE OBJECTIVES OF CANADA'S NATIONAL ENERGY PROGRAM

Overview

In his introduction to the NEP, the Honourable Marc Lalonde outlined the three objectives of the program:

1. "It must establish the basis for Canadians to seize control of their own energy future through *security* of supply and ultimate independence from the world oil market.
2. It must offer Canadians, all Canadians, the real *opportunity* to participate in the energy industry in general and the petroleum industry in particular, and to share in the benefits of industry expansion.
3. It must establish a petroleum pricing and revenue-sharing regime that recognizes the requirements of *fairness* to all Canadians no matter where they live."[3]

Looking upon these objectives in the context of the energy problem outlined in the preceding section, one can only conclude that, at most, a small fraction of the NEP is devoted to what would be commonly regarded as the national energy problem. And, while it is true that the control of the petroleum industry raises questions and indeed may be perceived by some as a problem, it is not an energy problem as such but rather relates to the difference between an ideal world and the world that we actually have. If one, for example, were to evaluate the NEP solely in terms of the way it comes to grips with Canada's energy problems, one would simply omit consideration of the various proisions of the program designed to achieve the opportunity and fairness objectives, preferring to treat those as arising from a broader political, social, even philosophical context.

We could do that if the pursuit of those objectives were unrelated to the likely attainment of the security objective. In fact, they are not. The burden of much of the discussion in this volume is that pursuit of objectives other than the security of energy supply, may jeopardize the attainment of the supply objective. But we will have more to say about this at a later stage. For now we want to turn our attention to the individual objectives that are articulated in the energy document and examine briefly how the program proposes to attain them.

A. SECURITY OF SUPPLY

The conservation game plan

Although security of supply is allegedly the principal objective of the NEP, the policy does not assume that there will be a supply solution to the energy problem. Somewhat surprisingly, given the recent effective stance of policy, the self-sufficiency objective is to be realized by 1990 via a reduction in oil consumption rather than any dramatic increase in domestic production. One of the principal methods for achieving the projected decline in oil consumption is the wholesale substitution of gas for oil. While this is expected to occur predominantly in the Maritimes, gasification will be encouraged in general industrial applications as well.

To achieve this substitution, a number of direct incentive programs have been proposed. For example, grants will be provided to encourage homeowners to adapt their heating systems to natural gas, electricity or biomass sources and to convert fleet trucks and cars from gasoline to propane. To ensure that heavy oil and residual fuel oils are used more effectively, incentives are provided for heavy oil upgrading in Western Canada and the capability for residual fuel oil cracking in Eastern Canada. In order to assist the Maritimes to convert to natural gas, a natural gas pipeline will be extended from Montreal to serve Eastern Quebec and the Maritimes. Research on the use of biomass and other renewable energy forms will be directly subsidized and the use of petroleum as a petrochemical feedstock will be actively discouraged in favour of natural gas or even coal.

In addition to these various programs to encourage substitution away from oil, a number of initiatives have been proposed to increase the extent to which Canadians are conservation conscious. Minimum miles-per-gallon automobile regulations and the continuation of the Canadian Home Insulation Program are joined by other initiatives in the industrial sector. For example, the principal conservation program in the industrial sector will take the form of funding "to double the number of government-industry seminars and workshops and to develop and deliver an employee motivation program for industry. An expanded energy audit program will be instituted . . . to assist industries and businesses to identify energy waste and plan corrective measures."[4]

B. FAIRNESS

A selective notion of equity

The NEP promises a fairness to "the consumer in terms of oil and gas prices, and in terms of the help provided by the Government of Canada to Canadians, so that they can play their part in achieving their energy goals; the producing provinces by ensuring that they enjoy substantial and growing revenues from their resources; and all Canadians, by providing the Government of Canada with the fiscal capacity to fulfill its national responsibilities."[5]

Harking back to our original comment about the reason for including the fairness and opportunity goals in the NEP, it is strange that no mention is made in the fairness objective of the individuals and corporations who have, during the course of the last several decades, employed their savings and their capital in the oil and gas industry. As is clear from subsequent discussion in this paper and the other papers in the volume, this is more than an incidental omission since the failure to consider fairness to providers of capital to the energy industry, be they foreigners or Canadians, will have a considerable impact on the extent to which the program achieves the security of supply objective.

The principal components of the fairness aspect of the NEP are subsidized prices to Canadian consumers, a redistribution of revenues away from the provincial governments and producing companies toward the Federal Government through a variety of taxation measures, and some attempt at regional redistribution of the federal revenues through a variety of expenditure programs. In view of the fact that other papers in this volume discuss the "fairness" objective, I will not deal with it here.

C. OPPORTUNITY

This objective which has been characterized as "Canadianization" and which I have elsewhere[6] described as "nationalization" of the industry, is potentially the most pervasive aspect of the energy program and the one with the most important long-term consequences. The main initiatives to ensure "opportunity" for Canadians are as follows: a minimum of 50 per cent Canadian participation in any production of oil or gas from "Canada Lands" (the Canadian north and off Canada's coasts); a 25 per cent carried interest or "confiscation right" for Petro-

Canada or some other Crown Corporation for any promising oil and gas developments in Canada Lands; at least 50 per cent Canadian ownership of oil and gas production by 1990; an early increase in the share of the oil and gas sector owned by the Government of Canada; discrimination against firms more than 25 per cent foreign-owned by reducing incentive payments for exploration and development expenditures of various types.

These then are the three pillars upon which the NEP rests. In the following sections we will analyze each of these pillars with the particular objective of ascertaining how they relate to the national energy problem as described in section one and describe what implications they may have in the broader economic arena.

IV. IMPLICATIONS OF THE NEP FOR CANADA'S ENERGY PROBLEM

A. HOW REALISTIC IS THE CONSERVATION GAME PLAN?

As noted, the NEP is essentially based on the notion that the solution to the national energy problem is conservation and substitution away from oil. Characterization of the end result of this process is summarized in the following figures taken from the NEP.[7]

OIL DEMAND AND SUPPLY OUTLOOK
(1000 barrels/day)

	1979	1985	1990
Production	1,608	1,355	1,520
Demand	1,823	1,615	1,475
Net Imports (Exports)	215	260	(45)

Source: NEP, p. 99.

The implication of this projected oil demand and supply outlook is that total oil consumption in Canada will decline by 11.4 per cent between 1979 and 1985. As noted, this will be achieved by a combination of substituting natural gas for oil and by direct reduction in the energy use in those sectors which are incapable of making this substitution.

It is obviously difficult to assess with any great precision, the extent to which these projections are likely to be fulfilled. However, we can get some idea by comparing this projected experience with the experience recorded during the six years following the dramatic escalation of oil prices in 1973.

Many industrial nations began immediately to cope with the problem of oil conservation by adapting their domestic prices to the changed world circumstances. As is well known, Canada was not one of those nations and, in fact, has pursued consistently a policy of insulating domestic consumers from the emerging reality of higher world oil prices, a policy which has, to some extent, led to the current difficulties. Lower prices have meant a continuation of growth in the demand for oil because energy-using practices which would have changed in the face of higher prices have not adjusted to the radically-changed world energy circumstances.

The percentage change in oil consumption in the six years between 1973 and 1979 for the major industrial countries was as follows: U.S.A. 6.8 per cent, Japan 3.4 per cent, Germany -1.1 per cent, France -5.0 per cent, U.K. -13.8 per cent, Italy 5.9 per cent, and Canada 10.6 per cent. Three out of seven of the major industrial countries have thus experienced increased energy consumption over the six year period since the initial escalation in oil prices and only the United Kingdom has been successful in achieving the sort of reduction in oil consumption which is projected for the next six years under the NEP. It is worthwhile noting that those countries which have achieved actual reductions in oil consumptions, have been those countries which immediately adapted their price structure to emerging world prices. It is also worth noting that Japan's positive growth in oil consumption, in spite of the world level prices, relates directly to Japan's overall economic growth which has far outstripped the growth rates in the other countries cited.

Given that the NEP does not provide for a rapid adjustment of Canadian oil prices toward world prices and that it specifically provides that Canada will never adjust completely to world oil prices, it must be noted with some skepticism that we are proposing to accomplish what only one of our major trading partners has been able to accomplish.

As noted, the countries who have had success in reducing their dependence on imported oil by reducing their oil consumption, are precisely those countries which have gone immediately to world price levels. A principal reason for discounting the achievement of the oil consumption targets laid down in the NEP is the fact that again Canada is explicitly eschewing a policy of world oil pricing. In fact, the real price of gasoline under the NEP will actually decline if one accepts the projections contained in the NEP as an accurate assessment of future trends.

Gasoline prices will decline in real terms

The blended price of crude oil to refiners is scheduled to increase by $4.50 per barrel per year for the period 1981 to 1983. If we assume that the increases in the price of crude oil are passed along to the products in the same proportions in which they are produced, then this $4.50 price rise will result in an increase of about 12.9 cents per gallon of gasoline. Given what this implies for percentage increases in the future in the price of gasoline, depends on which base price one utilizes in the calculation. It seems reasonable at this point in time to assume a base price of $1.30 per gallon which is the effective price of gasoline across the country at the end of December 1980. This price includes $1.75 Petroleum Compensation Charge which was given effect at the time of the budget, but does not include the first of the $4.50 increases in the price of a barrel of oil. Using the $1.30 per gallon base price, the NEP provides for an increase in the price of gasoline of 9.9 per cent in 1981, 9 per cent in 1982, and 8.3 per cent in 1983. These increases are less than the government's own forecast of inflation for those three years as provided for in the budget and, indeed, there is some reason at this juncture to believe that the government's forecasts of inflation are, in fact, very optimistic.

This likely falling real price of gasoline is the Achilles heel of the NEP from the point of view of achieving the sort of oil consumption reductions that are built into it. The fact is that 44 per cent of all petroleum is utilized in the transportation industry and unless significant conservation is induced in this sector, there seems almost no possibility to effect the 11.4 per cent reduction in petroleum usage projected in the NEP.

Of course, there is some possibility that refiners of petroleum would elect to pass more than 12.9 cents per gallon on to users in the transportation sector. However, that would not be characteristic. As is clear from Table III, petroleum used in the transportation sector has tended to increase in price less rapidly than fuel oil and other liquid fuels, natural gas, and coal and much less rapidly than other products of the distillation process such as heavy fuel oil.

TABLE III
CHANGES IN CANADIAN ENERGY PRICES, 1973-1979

	Per cent Change
Consumer Prices	
Motor Gasoline	87
Natural Gas	143
Fuel Oil & Other Liquid Fuel	152
Electricity	85
CPI	70
Industry Purchase Prices	
Thermal Coal	221
Electricity — over 5000 kw	127
— under 5000 kw	85
Industry Selling Prices	
Heavy Fuel Oil	296

Source: Statistics Canada, Cat. No. 62-001, 62-010 and 62-011.

An improbable goal

In part, the NEP recognizes Canadians' insatiable demand for energy and, in fact, projects a continuous 1.9 per cent growth per year in the extent of energy usage as far out as 1990. However, according to their calculation, oil's share is expected to fall from 43 per cent of total energy use in 1979 to only 27 per cent in 1990. As noted above, the primary means to this end is a massive substitution program away from oil toward natural gas. The probability of achieving this goal can be assessed in the context of the regional distribution figures mentioned above.

At present, for example, oil provides only 34 per cent of Alberta's energy needs. That is much lower than the 38 per cent utilized by Manitoba which has the second lowest oil share of any province as illustrated in Table II. Now, if the national objective of 27 per cent is to be realized, given that other areas of the country are inherently more dependent on oil, then at the very least Alberta's usage of oil would have to be reduced to the 27 per cent objective by 1990. However, at the present time Alberta has already undertaken a massive program of conversion to natural gas. It has subsidized natural gas consumption for several years and, hence, provided consumers with a real incentive to convert to natural gas. It has also undertaken a rural gasification program which on an uneconomic basis pipes gas to farms and settlements in sparcely settled rural areas. It hardly seems conceivable that Alberta can dramatically increase the extent to which natural gas is substituted for oil.

The conversion of the Maritime Provinces to natural gas would certainly decrease dependency on oil but given Alberta's limited success, in spite of its gasification program, in reducing the total fraction of oil in the energy bill, it seems highly unlikely that the oil intensity figure for the whole country can be reduced to the 27 per cent level projected in the NEP. There is an inherent presumption in the NEP that the extension of a natural gas pipeline to the Maritimes will, in some sense, automatically provide for the extent of gasification necessary to achieve the reduction in oil consumption. However, as should be clear from the case of Alberta where natural gas has been plentifully available, that is not the end of the story. Consumers have actually got to undertake the task of energy source conversion and that may or may not be done at a fast enough pace to achieve, in the Maritime Provinces, even the current national average of 45 per cent — let alone the more ambitious 27 per cent target.

One would have to conclude, on the basis of international experience with oil consumption and on the basis of domestic Canadian experience with gasification, that it will be very difficult to achieve the targets outlined in the NEP. Or, at least it will be difficult to achieve them given the program of policies proposed.

B. HOW SECURE IS SUPPLY?

An ambitious program of construction

The other hope for dealing effectively with the incipient shortage of petroleum arises on the supply side of the equation, that is, that we may expand production at a faster pace than the demand increases. Unfortunately, although supply expansion may under some circumstances have provided relief from the incipient shortages, the NEP provides no prospect of a remedy from that source. The authors of the NEP, in fact, explicitly assume, along with other observers, that production from conventional reserves in Western Canada will continue to decline. In the short run, this decline will have to be offset by increased imports. Toward the latter part of the decade, however, the NEP optimistically projects that increased production from non-conventional sources will more than make up the declining production from Western Canada. The projections made in the NEP include explicitly the following additional production facilities and start-up dates for non-conventional oil projects: Suncor expansion (1982-83); Syncrude expansion (1985-86); Cold Lake Project (1987); Alsands Project (1987); and Petro-Canada-Nova Project (1990-1991).

As with the assessment of the NEP's optimistic view of conservation and substitution, there is room for considerable skepticism about the projected supplies of synthetic oil. Simultaneous completion of the mega-projects, for example, will put a very heavy strain on the construction industry in Alberta as well as on the supplies of manpower and essential materials from elsewhere in the country. There is reason, therefore, to be uncomfortable about the certainty with which the proposed schedules can be met. In the particular case of the Alsands and Cold Lake projects, the impasse between the Federal Government and the Alberta Government has, at the time of this writing, led to these operations being put on hold with unknown consequence for the projected time of completion.

The cost of delay and dispute

Quite apart from the fact that the delay of the synthetic oil plants will jeopardize the continuity of future oil supplies, it will also prove to be quite expensive. Any shortfall of domestic production, whether because of delays or because of future cutbacks in Alberta production, will have to be made up by foreign imports. Assuming 1987 oil import prices of $60 per barrel, a very conservative figure, a one year delay in the Alsands and Cold Lake projects would add over $6 billion to the oil import bill for that year. Moreover, delay in these projects could jeopardize the completion of the other synthetic oil plants because of construction bottlenecks. If this were to happen, the cumulative cost of delay could be enormous.

Alberta's announced cutbacks in oil production will add $1.7 billion to the oil import bill in 1981. Should the cutbacks continue through 1982 the total cost would escalate to $2.6 billion.

Orphaned conventional oil

One unambiguous thread in the NEP is its focus on frontier oil and synthetics. Secondary and tertiary recovery from existing wells and the discovery of new conventional wells in the Alberta region are, in effect, relatively discouraged by the budget. And, while the big payoff in terms of future supplies will undoubtedly come from the synthetics and the frontier oil pools, the fact is that Canada will face an increasingly severe domestic oil supply shortage between now and the mid to late part of the 1980s when these supplies will be available. Other authors in this volume argue on technical grounds that this is not a wise course of action in view of the fact that it amounts to putting our collective energy eggs in what has proven to be a very fragile basket.

While simple prudence would suggest that no available source of oil be intentionally deleted from the menu of possibilities, there are apparently straightforward, mechanical reasons for not abandoning the conventional sources. These mechanical requirements have to do with the rate at which primary recovery from existing oil pools occurs.

The standard projections of the output profile from conventional oil pools assumes that at various stages in the process of exploiting the oil, there will be a program of "in-fill" drilling. The objective of this drilling is to speed up the primary recovery rate. Failure to engage in this secondary drilling program slows the rate of production — in some cases by as much as 10 per cent per year.

The projections of conventional oil supply capability contained in the NEP assume that such "in-fill" drilling will occur. Many firms in the industry have already decided that the provisions of the NEP make such a drilling program economically infeasible. To the extent that this occurs on a widespread basis, the conventional oil supply projections contained in the NEP will prove to be too optimistic and the crude oil deficit will be correspondingly larger than is currently anticipated.

In fairness to the NEP, it should be noted that its provisions are merely the last straw rather than the total load which will extinguish much of the conventional oil exploration activity. The existing level of royalties imposed by the Alberta government before the NEP was widely regarded as excessive — especially by comparison with taxation imposed on exploration in the generally less productive areas in the United States. Thus, while it may serve the interests of Western apologists to lay the blame for the current difficulties at Ottawa's door, some of the responsibility must surely rest with the governments in the producing provinces.

Canadianization will inhibit security of supply

A number of other provisions of the NEP relating to the Canadianization and fairness objectives will also have unfortunate consequences for the security of supply. First of all, the Canadianization initiatives will likely serve to hinder technology transfer which has important implications for the crucial heavy oil and tar sands developments. The technology related to both these areas is not well understood and these projects are very much on the frontier of technology. Experimentation with enhanced or tertiary recovery techniques for heavy oils is more advanced in the United States than in Canada. By discouraging foreign-owned oil companies from engaging in such activities, Canada will presumably find it more difficult to tap this body of knowledge.

In the past, access to foreign technology and foreign expertise has proved to be essential in the development of Canadian projects. For example, when the Syncrude plant was experiencing production difficulties after its initial start-up, it was a team of scientists and engineers from Exxon in the United States which came to Canada to help solve the problems. It is reasonable to inquire as to whether or not such teams of experts will be available to help 75 per cent Canadian-owned consortia. Against this position it is often argued that it is more important for Canada to develop and have the rights to her technology because with that technology in hand the enormous hydrocarbon reserves of the tar sands will be a unique world-scale resource. While one can have some sympathy with this point of view, it is appropriate to ask whether or not the cost in terms of petroleum shortfalls that may arise as a consequence, may not be more extensive than Canadians would want to bear if they had the choice.

V. THE NATIONAL ENERGY PROGRAM IN HISTORICAL PERSPECTIVE

A broader set of concerns

While the Canadian oil and gas industry is probably one of the most regulated sectors in the economy, it is nevertheless the case that the NEP can be viewed as an attempt to provide the Canadian federal government with a more direct hands-on management of the Canadian energy sector. As has already been pointed out, there are a number of reasons to believe that the process of achieving this control may in fact jeopardize the solution to our energy problems proper. It therefore seems reasonable to inquire as to why the NEP was adopted and why it contains such a pervasive extension of control over an already heavily controlled industry. In order to answer this question, it is necessary to consider a broader set of issues and, in particular, to review the history of political concern about foreign domination and control of Canadian industry during the last several decades.

The philosophical issues

The NEP was launched against a backdrop of widespread belief that the Canadian oil and gas industry is completely dominated by foreign interests and moreover that this situation was becoming more serious as time passed. As a political stratagem responding to this general perception, the NEP is simply the latest in a long series of public and private initiatives aimed at wresting control of Canadian industry from foreign dominance. As early as 1957, for example, the Gordon Commission drew public attention to the evils of foreign ownership and the means to end it.

The set of issues involved can perhaps best be summarized by a series of remarks by, now Prime Minister then private citizen, Pierre Elliot Trudeau, writing in a well-publicized article in *Cité Libre* in 1958. In that article Mr. Trudeau posed the following question: "Can Canada free herself from the domination exercised by foreigners, particularly Americans, on our economy?" His reply, which provides insight to the mentality which infuses the NEP, was as follows:

> Apart from the exclusion, pure and simple, of American capital, a perfectly reactionary solution which would assume a vigorous braking of our economic expansion and radical reduction of our standard of living, two attitudes remain possible: either we shall passively suffer one situation of economic domination, and then it

would be better to be annexed outright to the United States, rather than be a colony exploited without limit. Or else we shall intervene vigorously in the game of economic forces by adopting economic policies which take into account the following factors:

- The gradual exhaustion of American resources, as stated in the Paley report.
- The monopoly held in Canada on certain resources.
- The pressing need that Americans have of finding markets for their surpluses of production and capital.
- The existence of such markets in Canada, which unite conditions of economic profitability and political security with rare good fortune.

These facts give Canada a bargaining power which would allow her to direct capital according to the following priorities:

Social profitability must take precedence over economic profitability: houses, schools and hospitals must come before factories and mills . . .

The resources which cannot be preserved, before those which can wait, until we need them without dwindling; for example, waterfalls and forests before oil and mines . . .

He further added:

it would not always be a misfortune if we turned foreign capital away from time to time towards countries less demanding and less fortunate than ours.[8]

While it would be simplistic to suppose that these views of the Prime Minister were the single motivating force behind the development of a variety of subsequent policy adventures, it is nevertheless the case that the broad thrust of government policy in the period of the various Trudeau governments has reflected this general policy thrust. The Foreign Investment Review Agency was established in 1972, Petro-Canada in 1976, The Canadian Petroleum Monitoring Survey conducted under the authority of the *Petroleum Corporation Monitoring Act* passed in June 1978, the Canadian Petroleum Monitoring Agency in August 1980, and now most recently, the National Energy Program in October 1980.

In the light of this philosophical progression it is perhaps not surprising that the protest that the NEP will inhibit the attainment of energy security falls upon deaf ears. The principal concern of those who share the views articulated so clearly by Mr. Trudeau in 1958, is that policy provide a concrete expression of nationalism and not that it optimize economic efficiency.

Further insight into the NEP is provided by considering the historical developments in the industry itself.

The industry's development

It was not until the discovery of the Leduc oil field in 1947 that Canada acquired the capability to become a significant oil producer. However, in those early days the oil from Alberta was relatively more expensive than the increasingly abundant supplies from Venezuela and the Middle East. Because of its higher cost, Alberta oil was not attractive for users.

In order to create a market for Alberta oil in the East the Conservative-appointed Borden Commission recommended in 1957 that an artificial commercial barrier be erected along the Ottawa Valley. All markets west of this so-called Borden Line would be serviced by Alberta oil and all oil consumption to the East would be serviced by the somewhat cheaper imported oil. This initiative resulted in more than a doubling of Western Canadian domestic oil production from 450,000 barrels per day in 1958 to over 1,000,000 barrels per day in 1968. But even this dramatic increase in market fell short of Alberta's capacity to produce and by 1968 over 600,000 barrels of oil per day were being shut-in. This amount of excess production capability almost identically matched the extent of imports to Eastern Canada from foreign supplies at that time.

At the same time, dramatic developments were occurring in the rest of the oil-producing world. In 1950 the U.S. had produced about one-half of total world production but by 1960 this figure was reduced to one-third and a decade later to less than 20 per cent. By 1972 conventional oil production in the United States peaked and with demand continuing to increase, the shortfall was satisfied with Canadian exports which rose to approximately 1,000,000 barrels per day by 1972.

In the maelstrom created by the world oil shortage in 1973-74 and the consequent rapid rise in world oil prices, the Federal Energy Minister, Mr. Macdonald informed the United States in 1973 that, henceforth, Canada was going to price its oil exports at world prices. The justification for this move was that Canada was having to pay those same world prices for its imports. He further indicated that Canada would be phasing out completely its oil export program within 10 to 15 years. Moreover, he warned the United States that they could not count on massive development in the Athabasca Tar Sands since such development when it did take place, would be geared to Canadian needs. He also indicated that Canadian gas exports, which reached a record level in 1973, were to become much more expensive to reflect world prices of petroleum.

Inter-governmental disputes

In 1974 Mr. Macdonald enunciated the government's first comprehensive policy directed at long-term energy self-reliance within Canada. This policy, amongst other things, included a $2.40 per barrel increase in oil prices to the then staggering level of $6.50 per barrel — a level still considerably below the world price. The immediate question that arose out of this increased price of oil was "Who was to get the extra revenue?"

Alberta, for its part, announced an increased royalty that would effectively capture 65 per cent of the increased domestic price. Under the federal *Income Tax Act* these royalties had been deductible historically for corporate income tax purposes. With no change in the tax regime, the net effect of the 65 per cent Alberta royalty would have been to reduce the tax revenue of the federal government while at the same time increasing the expenditure requirements of the federal government in the form of the higher equalization payments necessary to equalize the tax yield across the provinces. Federal response was to make the new higher provincial royalties non-deductible for federal income tax purposes.

The end result was a total tax impact on the oil industry that, in some cases, exceeded 100 per cent and, not surprisingly, the industry responded by rapidly curtailing its activities. The impact on oil exploration was clearly reflected in the stock market as Canadian oil share prices fell over 50 per cent. The grass roots sentiments associated with this cutback in activity were reflected in the popular Alberta bumper sticker of the day "Will the last person to leave please turn out the lights?"

In the face of this clear evidence that they had gone too far and because the industry's actions clearly threatened potential tax revenue to both the Alberta and federal governments, both modified their proposals and introduced incentives to bring the industry back. Higher wellhead prices and an attractive set of exploration incentives ultimately succeeded in restoring exploration activity to the level which it had been achieving prior to the royalties impasse.

A re-run of recent history?

Clearly the events of 1980 bear striking resemblance to those of 1974-75. The Alberta and federal governments are again locked in a battle over revenues and once again industry finds itself in an unattractive, perhaps even hostile, political environment and faces uncertain economic prospects. Unlike 1974-75, however, the federal government's position in 1980 seems to be considerably firmer and, indeed, its objectives more clearly defined than was the case in 1974-75. Another difference between the situation in 1980 and that which existed in 1974-75 is the fact that exploration and development in the United States has been made much more attractive by the fact that world price equivalents are being offered on new oil discoveries in the United States. Even before the NEP was promulgated, many Canadian exploration firms had been moving their operations to the United States to take advantage of the higher yields.

VI. THE CANADIANIZATION OBJECTIVE

A. THE FACTS ABOUT FOREIGN OWNERSHIP AND CONTROL

As we have noted in several cases, the objective of Canadianization of the oil and gas industry is a pervasive undercurrent in the NEP. Indeed, it may be one of the principal motivations for the whole NEP and in some instances has been shown to override what, in our view, should be the more pressing concern of energy security. Because it does play such a crucial role in the program, it behooves us to consider more carefully the facts about foreign ownership and control and the implications of the Canadianization objective.

Government documents related to energy, speak about ownership and control in a variety of ways related to revenue, assets, production and sales. Depending upon the argument being advanced, one or more of these concepts may be chosen. For example, the 1979 Canadian Petroleum Industry Monitoring Survey states:

> Foreign ownership of the total production of oil and gas in 1979 declined two points to 68.7 per cent while foreign control at 77.2 per cent was down some four points from the previous year . . . Similar declines are registered in foreign ownership and control on the industry's total revenue. These levels stood at 72.0 per cent and 81.7 per cent respectively in 1979.[9]

The figures cited in this quotation differ markedly from those recently published by Statistics Canada and reproduced here in Table IV. According to Statistics Canada:

> Foreign-owned capital in the petroleum and natural gas industry at 1976 year-end fell to 51 per cent from 54 per cent, at 1975 year-end. United States-controlled investment in this industry declined by five percentage points to 54 per cent while that controlled by residents of other countries declined to 14 per cent from 15 per cent. Projected estimates for petroleum and natural gas indicate that control by United States' residents fell by four percentage points in 1977 and a further eight percentage points to 42 per cent at 1978 year-end.[10]

TABLE IV
CONTROL OF CAPITAL EMPLOYED IN THE PETROLEUM AND NATURAL GAS INDUSTRY

	Percentage of Investment Controlled in			Percentage of Capital Employed Controlled in		
	Canada	United States	Other Countries	Canada	United States	Other Countries
1969	2.9	6.8	1.7	26	60	14
1970	3.0	7.5	1.9	24	61	15
1971	3.2	8.3	2.2	23	61	16
1972	3.9	8.6	2.4	26	58	16
1973	4.1	9.6	2.7	25	59	16
1974	4.4	10.5	2.8	25	59	16
1975	5.1	11.8	3.0	26	59	15
1976	7.4	12.6	3.1	32	54	14
1977	n/a	n/a	n/a	36	50	14
1978	n/a	n/a	n/a	45	42	13

n/a not available
Source: Statistics Canada, Cat. No. 11-001.

The figures by year-end 1980 will show a continuing decline in U.S. control of capital investment in the industry, reflecting the continuing pre-budget growth of Canadian interest in the industry.

Notwithstanding the popular impression about foreign ownership of the petroleum industry and the view which the NEP is pleased to encourage, several facts must be clearly recognized.

Canadian ownership was increasing before the NEP

The first fact that must be acknowledged is that whatever figures one chooses to use, there has been a dramatic trend towards increased Canadian ownership and control in the oil and gas industry. Moreover, this trend is continuing.

Government energy documents are selective in data use

The second point, and this is not evident from the data, is that energy-related government documents arbitrarily exclude from their computation of foreign ownership, all energy pipeline and distribution system companies. These companies are predominantly Canadian-owned and constitute a substantial fraction of total investment in the industry. Consequently, their omission from the statistics imparts a distortive upward bias to the calculation of the extent of foreign ownership. No reason is given for excluding the pipeline and distribution companies from the determination of ownership.

Measurements of ownership distorted

The third point is that the choice of ownership criterion greatly affects the impression given by the figures. In the case, for example, of capital ownership, the government argument is cast in terms of the ownership of "voting shares". In attributing ownership on the basis of voting shares, the government calculations group debt instruments and other classes of shares together with the majority voting shares. This, in spite of the fact that the debt instruments and other classes of shares may well have a prior claim on the assets of the company! Evidently this procedure arbitrarily increases the measured amount of foreign ownership registered in the figures.

The use of revenues and/or production as an index of Canadian ownership also biases the statistics in favour of the federal government's argument. This is so because most of the revenue and most of the production currently being generated by the industry arises from the major integrated companies which are largely foreign-owned. The staggering number of Canadian oil companies which have been formed over recent years and which are as yet in the early stages of their development as producers and earners of revenue, are not included in the statistics if either production or revenues are used as the basis for the ownership calculation. Moreover, to the extent that Canadian oil companies sell their oil to the major integrated companies, Canadian-controlled production would show up as part of the revenues of a foreign-owned firm.

It clearly seems to be the case that the Statistics Canada figures, which show actual capital ownership in the industry, are likely to be a more reliable index of foreign ownership. The figures yielded by the Statistics Canada surveys show that only about 40 per cent of the industry is in fact controlled in the United States and not 70 or 80 per cent as is implied by other figures selectively used by the authors of various government energy documents. More importantly, the conclusion to be reached from the various forms of data are very different. In the case of the Statistics Canada data the conclusion would be that under the circumstances existing prior to the NEP, foreign ownership in the industry was declining, indeed rapidly declining, and it would certainly not have indicated the need for any major policy initiatives with regard to ownership, given the threat that such initiatives might pose for the achievement of the goal of energy security. The revenue and production figures cited in government energy related documents, on the other hand, show nearly twice the level of foreign control as is evidenced in the actual capital ownership data and would be much more the source of a cause for concern to those who give Canadian ownership a high priority.

B. WILL CANADIANIZATION MEAN NATIONALIZATION?

There seems ample justification for questioning the basis upon which the authors of the NEP have concluded that a major Canadianization initiative is necessary at this time. Since that initiative has been taken, however, we have to accept it as an on-going objective of government policy whether justified or not. The issue then arises as to whether or not the NEP taken as a package is likely to encourage Canadianization of the industry via the private sector or whether the program will involve an even greater participation by government in the sector.

Taken as a whole, the NEP, as we have noted before, represents a major, new thrust by government into the energy sector. By and large, in the future, industry returns will be lower, the industry will be more heavily regulated, and the prospects are for increasing amounts of regulation and taxation. This combination of regulation and taxation is likely to produce a very low return on capital invested in the industry as well as increasing the uncertainty which will be associated with that lower return. One can legitimately ask whether or not this set of circumstances is likely to enhance the attractiveness of the energy sector for potential Canadian investors. The answer seems to unambiguously be that it will not and that, as a consequence, increasingly capital inflows to the industry will have to come from non-private sources.

Against this gloomy perspective, the NEP provides the promise of greater returns for investment in frontier areas if the Canadian content regulations are fulfilled. Supporters of the program claim that this will entice more Canadian capital into the industry. Moreover, it is claimed that in the case of synthetic fuel developments, the operators are guaranteed an attractive rate of return and hence there should be no reason, based on risk and uncertainty, for private investors to shy away from energy investments.

Whether this latter extension is sincere or not is best left to psychoanalysts. However, the NEP has established a principle which clearly casts into doubt the extent to which the dispensations of government can be reliably predicted. For example, the program provides for a 25 per cent retroactive participation by the federal government in developable oil discoveries in the frontier areas and also provides for a suspension of the agreement with Suncor that output from the Suncor plant would receive world price. The justification for the latter initiative is that the capital in place has been paid for and continued payment of world prices would merely result in "excessive profits". In the case of frontier developments, it is said that the oil companies knew that the federal government would, at some point, exercise some form of "back-in" rights with regard to frontier development.

Whatever the justification for these arbitrary changes in the conditions under which the industry operates, it can be said with certainty that the force of these examples will not be lost on potential investors. Moreover, the attitude of investors has already been reflected in the share prices of various Canadian and foreign corporations and the total value of energy shares had dropped by more than $4 billion in the weeks following the budget announcement.

There is also a technical reason why the NEP will be relatively unsuccessful in augmenting Canadianization, at least in the short run. As noted above, many Canadian-owned corporations are in the early stages of their development and invest most of their energies and money in the process of exploration and, hence, are much more mobile than the large, integrated multi-nationals who have large amounts of capital invested in production and distribution facilities. As a consequence, the overall negative impact of the NEP on the future prospects for the industry, will be reflected in an out-migration of the smaller, mobile firms. This process has been dramatically documented by the exodus of such phenomenally successful Canadian corporations as Hunter Explorations. In other words, the very firms which the NEP seeks to encourage have been the first and will be the most numerous to leave the country because of the impact of the program.

Is socialization the real goal?

The point is that the net impact of the NEP has been to make the petroleum sector a relatively unattractive area for investment and consequently that additional flows of capital to the industry will have to come from other than private sources. To the extent that government is the provider of this capital, the Canadianization objective might better be described as nationalization or socialization rather than Canadianization.

C. THE COST OF CANADIANIZATION

There seems ample reason to believe that the Canadianization objective will not, in fact, be achieved via the private sector. Recent estimates of the cost to the Canadian government of achieving this self-imposed Canadian ownership objective directly, have ranged from between $10 billion to $18 billion. The NEP contains explicit provision for a takeover tax to finance this major acquisitions program. The takeover tax would evidence itself by higher prices at the pump and total expenditures by consumers on energy products would have to dramatically increase. If the nationalization route to Canadianization is adopted, however, the $10 to $18 billion employed to that end would contribute absolutely nothing toward the attainment of the oil security goal which should, in our view, be the pre-eminent concern of the NEP.

Quite apart from the fact that this massive expenditure would not contribute toward the discovery of a single, extra barrel of oil, the initiative raises real questions about public choice which cannot be ignored. As noted, the other provisions of the NEP are likely to make investment in the Canadian petroleum industry very unattractive. If that is true and Canadian investors decide to invest their capital in other countries simply because the prospects there are more attractive, on what basis is it that the federal government can claim to represent the interests of Canadians in forcing the allocation of Canadian capital toward the acquisition of assets in the Canadian petroleum industry?

VII. SUMMARY AND CONCLUSIONS

In the Introduction we indicated that the NEP should be viewed as a broad, political and social initiative on the part of government, rather than as a strictly economic undertaking. In examining each of the major pieces of the NEP it becomes clear that assessment is accurate.

Solving the energy problem

The national energy problem was found to involve increasing energy deficits on an international trade basis and uncertainties regarding future supply on a domestic basis. The NEP was found to be ineffectual in dealing with this basic problem. The conservation targets assumed in the package were found to be unrealistic both from the point of view of oil consumption reduction and the natural gas substitution. The fundamental weakness in the program was found to be the failure to move more rapidly to world prices of oil.

The supply projections contained in the program were also found to be optimistic and in light of the program's general provisions, unlikely to be achieved.

Canadianization

The factual basis upon which the government has launched its major Canadianization initiative was found to be selective and incomplete. Careful consideration of recent Statistics Canada data suggested that only about half the capital employed in the Canadian petroleum sector is foreign-owned and that this fraction was rapidly declining. There seems to be no independent reason for a major Canadianization initiative at this time, other than as the expression of a system of value judgements which were traced to the Gordon Commission of 1957 and the writings of, then private citizen, P.E. Trudeau. The pursuit of the Canadianization objective was found, in many instances, to be incompatible with the energy security goal and an obstacle to its achievement.

Because of the various effects of the program, the Canadianization objective will probably involve much more direct government ownership of the industry at tremendous cost in terms of capital and foregone supply development.

Value judgements

One would like to believe that the NEP will solve the country's energy problem. The conclusion which we must draw, however, is that it will not. Moreover, the overall assessment of the program must be that it is the expression of a judgement to the effect that "who owns the capital employed in the industry? and who benefits from its deployment?" are more important questions than whether or not Canadians will have a continuously available supply of oil. While many Canadians have expressed concern about ownership and benefit, it is not clear they would place that concern above the vital issue of oil supply. Nor is it clear that they would willingly tolerate, if they were aware of them, the shortages and/or the system of rationing that the future may hold because of the NEP's failure to confront the very real problems of future supply.

FOOTNOTES

1 Government of Canada, Energy, Mines and Resources. *The National Energy Program*. (1980), p. 1.
2 See for example Z.C. Slagorsky, *Energy Use in Canada in Comparison With Other Countries*, Canadian Energy Research Institute (1979).
3 *Op. cit.*, p. 2.
4 *Ibid.*, p. 72.
5 *Ibid.*, p. 105-106.
6 *Financial Post*, November 22, 1980. p. 19.
7 *Op. cit.*, p. 99.
8 P.E. Trudeau, "The Economic Domination of Canada" in *Cité Libre*, (May 1958) and extracted in *Corporate Canada*, M. Starowicz and R. Murphy (eds.), James, Lewis and Samuel (1972).
9 Government of Canada, Energy, Mines and Resources. *Canadian Petroleum Monitoring Survey*, (1979).
10 Statistics Canada, *Statistics Canada Daily*, (November 24, 1980), p. 5.

Chapter 2

Canadian Energy Policy: Financing Our Energy Future

J.G. STABBACK
Vice President and Head
DARYLL G. WADDINGHAM
Senior Economic Advisor
Energy and Mineral Resource Department
Global Energy Group
Royal Bank of Canada
Calgary

THE AUTHOR

JACK GARRY STABBACK — Following graduation from the University of Alberta in 1949 with a Degree in Chemical Engineering, Mr. Stabback joined the Oil and Gas Conservation Board of the Province of Alberta (now the Energy Resources Conservation Board) as Field Engineer, later occupying the positions of Chief Gas Engineer, and Administrator for Gas.

In 1964 he was on loan to the Government of South Australia as a Technical Adviser, and in November of that year was appointed to the National Energy Board, where he served successively as Chief Engineer, Member of the Board, Associate Vice-Chairman, Vice-Chairman, and Chairman.

Mr. Stabback retired from the Board at the end of April 1980 and on June 1st was appointed a vice-president and head of the Energy and Mineral Resource Department within the Royal Bank's new Global Energy Group, with headquarters in Calgary.

Mr. Stabback was recently honoured as the first recipient of a new award of the Association Pipeline Longitude 75° of Montreal; and the recipient of the Selwyn Blaylock Medal for 1980, awarded by the Canadian Institute of Mining and Metallurgy.

THE AUTHOR

DARYLL G. WADDINGHAM has a B.A. and an M.A. in Economics from the University of New Brunswick specializing in the fields of Finance, Monetary Theory, and Econometrics. He has taken special course work in Econometrics at the Massachusetts Institute of Technology, Cambridge, Massachusetts. He was an Economic Advisor to the Province of New Brunswick from 1963 to 1967 and from 1967 to 1972, he served as a Research Officer in the Bank of Canada, Ottawa. For the next two years, he was Senior Underwriter, Government Finance, Dominion Securities Corporation/Harris & Partners Ltd., Toronto. In 1974 he became Senior Economist, Financial Economics, The Royal Bank of Canada and from mid-1978 to the present, he has been exclusively involved in energy research at the bank. Recently, he has completed a special balance of payments impact study of the Polar Gas project (a 2,300 mile pipeline from the Arctic Islands).

Mr. Waddingham is a member of the Canadian Economics Association, a past-president of the Montreal Economics Association and a founder of the Canadian Association for Business Economics. At The Royal Bank, Mr. Waddingham's responsibilities have encompassed financial market analysis and forecasting, central bank policy, funds flow research, and balance of payments research. He is a specialist in the area of government and utility finance. His present duties revolve around the energy and major project sector.

Canadian Energy Policy: Financing Our Energy Future*

J.G. STABBACK
Vice President and Head
DARYLL G. WADDINGHAM
Senior Economic Advisor
Energy and Mineral Resource Department
Global Energy Group
Royal Bank of Canada
Calgary

I. INTRODUCTION — SOME BACKGROUND

We all know that Canada is an enormous energy storehouse. The exact dimensions are not known, but the country's energy potential is very large in virtually every major sector — oil, gas, coal, uranium and hydro-electric power. At the present time, the bulk of this energy is potential energy in the sense that currently much of this energy has not been harnessed and remains at least several years away from the market. This is especially true of much of our coal reserves and unconventional and frontier oil. International energy events, particularly the rapid escalation of prices and the growing insecurity of supply, have enhanced the value of Canadian energy reserves and have accelerated the need for their development. The rise in international energy prices has also greatly increased Canada's economically recoverable reserves of energy and, in our view there are a great number of attractions to the rapid development of our energy resources.

*A shorter version of this paper was presented at the 1980 Outlook Conference Sponsored by the Association of Professional Economists of British Columbia, Vancouver, November 18, 1980. The authors are pleased to acknowledge the assistance of Christopher L. Fong and Geoffrey A. Cumming.

First of all, it appears clear that if Canada were to pursue an earnest development program of our national energy reserves we could produce an investment boom which would propel the country out of the existing unsatisfactory level of capital and labour utilization. Secondly, full-scale development could result in Canadian energy self-sufficiency in every sector, including crude oil, possibly as early as 1990. Personally, we are not wedded to the idea of complete self-sufficiency if other objectives such as regional balance and price stability are jeopardized. However, in light of the insecurity of international supply and the potential benefits to Canada, we believe Canada should pursue an aggressive, co-ordinated energy development program. Thirdly, the realization of Canada's energy potential would permit this country to supply greater volumes of energy to our energy-short allies and trading partners south of the border, in Europe and in the Far East. The importance of Canada's potential contribution to these countries should not be overlooked.

The energy trade balance

At the moment, Canada is a net energy exporter of uranium, coal, natural gas, petroleum products and electricity. In 1979, Canada's net energy trade balance amounted to somewhat more than $4 billion and there certainly is ample room for expansion.

With regard to crude oil, however, the situation is quite different from the general energy picture. In fact, the basic energy problem which we face in Canada is the deteriorating supply-demand balance in the crude oil sector. Last year, Eastern Canada imported more than half a million barrels of oil per day, of which 97 per cent was received from countries which are members of OPEC. Of this, 38 per cent was received from Persian Gulf producers. The Iranian revolution and the current Iranian-Iraqi hostilities have demonstrated the insecure nature of this supply. Furthermore, the landed price of this oil is about $35 per barrel and this constitutes a heavy drain on our balance of payments. The fact that our oil production is located in Western Canada, while the Atlantic region is wholly dependent upon insecure imported oil exacerbates our oil problem.

The domestic supply of oil

On the issue of domestic oil supply, light crude production is expected to decline rapidly during this decade. The rapidity of the decline will depend on the rate of future reserve additions from new discoveries and upon enhanced recovery from existing reserves, both of which are at least partially dependent upon the domestic price. Two years ago, the National Energy Board reported that light crude oil production would decline by approximately 55 per cent during the 1980s. A new review is now underway, but it is unlikely that this situation will be found to have changed substantially.

Heavy crude oil, Arctic and east coast oil and additional synthetic oil from the tar sands will all have a role to play in arresting the overall decline in our oil production, a role which could be quite large by 1990. The ultimate contribution non-conventional sources will make to Canadian supply will depend largely upon the investment climate. Needless to say, that climate is substantially influenced by government energy policy. Even in the most accommodative policy environment these additional sources will not contribute significantly to our oil supply before 1985 at the very earliest.

It is clear, then, that the years from now until the late 1980s will be insecure and uncertain for Canada in terms of crude oil supply.

The policy climate — the clash of legitimate interests

In Canada, energy policy-making and development are complicated, as we all are much too well aware, by constitutional provisions which result in split jurisdiction over energy resource management. In a broad country such as Canada shared jurisdiction, which prevents undue centralization or decentralization, of power may in the long run be quite advantageous, particularly if accompanied by a healthy dose of compromise as has been very much part of the Canadian political tradition. The present inter-governmental energy impasse is a very serious situation and we certainly hope that a satisfactory compromise can be achieved which will benefit all parties involved and permit the full development of Canada's energy potential.

An important reason for the inter-governmental energy dispute is that formerly somewhere between 70 and 80 per cent of energy revenues collected by Canadian governments accrued to the provincial governments, principally Alberta, and not to the federal government.† The federal government does have large expenditure requirements including transfer payments to the provinces, costs associated with subsidizing imported oil into Eastern Canada, and the cost of sponsoring various energy related programs. The provinces, for their part, are

†Editor's Note: For a different view of energy revenue shares see the paper by Professor Kenneth Norrie in this volume.

witnessing the rapid depletion of their non-renewable oil heritage and are, justifiably we believe, anxious to set aside sufficient financial resources to ensure a prosperous, diversified future once their oil reserves are depleted.

The recent federal budget is an attempt to redress the former revenue sharing arrangement and, if imposed, would substantially tilt the balance towards the federal government. The Alberta government has responded in a firm but measured manner. As a result of these competing moves, the inter-governmental struggle for shares of the energy pie has intensified and one is tempted to say that only the crust will be left for actual energy producers but that would be an exaggeration. In the remainder of this paper we consider the National Energy Program and some of its implications.

II. THE NATIONAL ENERGY PROGRAM (NEP)

First of all we must candidly admit that the program is so far-reaching and novel that it is difficult to accurately pinpoint the future impact on Canada, and we can make no sure claim that we have yet appreciated the full implications of it. Nevertheless, some effects on both the demand for and supply of oil are clear. The papers by M. Walker and C. Watkins in this volume consider the demand effects in some detail so we will restrict our comments to the supply side.

A. SUPPLY EFFECTS

The impact on capital

On the supply side, the NEP does not appear promising. Best guess-estimates are that by 1985, net Canadian oil imports will total approximately 600,000 barrels per day or 30 per cent of the country's requirements. Taxing the cash-flow of the industry and putting foreign firms operating in Canada to a disadvantage, which the NEP will do, are measures unlikely to enhance Canada's supply capability.

The critical need for capital

In Canada, the accelerating trend of energy investments witnessed since the mid-1970s will not only continue but will likely accelerate as Canada develops more costly conventional and non-conventional (including frontier) sources of energy. Over the past five years, coal and uranium investments have grown more quickly than either investment in crude oil and natural gas or the electrical utility industry. Electrical utilities have accounted for over 60 per cent of total energy spending in Canada. In the future, energy investments as a proportion of GNP will reach well over 9 per cent by the 1990s — more than double the experience of the late 1970s.

The fastest growing sector will be oil and gas, followed closely by related pipeline transportation system developments. Electrical generation will still be the largest segment of investment but its growth will slow down relative to the highly expansionary years of the 1960s and 1970s. In our opinion, energy investment will be, indeed, must be, the dominant component of fixed capital formation in Canada for the remainder of the century. In current dollar terms, our estimate is for energy spending in the order of $1.4 trillion over the next 20 years. About $530 billion of this total will represent conventional and frontier petroleum and coal mining industry development. Within that sum, $100 billion could easily be absorbed by oil sands and heavy oil projects. Natural gas distribution could consume another $80 billion. Pipeline projects are projected to require in excess of $80 billion and electrical utilities, the largest user of capital, are projected to require over $700 billion. Electrical generation and the petroleum sectors account for nearly 89 per cent of investment needs while pipelines account for the remainder.

To put these amounts in perspective, in the pre-OPEC era, between 1960 and 1974, total Canadian energy investment averaged about $2.5 billion per year. In the decade ahead, the annual average will be more than ten times larger. These are overwhelming sums for any economy, but are especially onerous requirements for a country with a population approaching 24 million and a current Gross National Product of $280 billion.

Sources of energy finance

Not all of this staggering amount of $1.4 trillion will have to be raised in the capital markets of Canada and abroad, for a significant portion of this investment could be funded internally by energy companies. In Canada, petroleum and natural gas companies have historically raised 70 to 85 per cent of their capital needs from internal sources. At the other extreme, electric utilities have raised only 30 per cent of their funds internally. Because of the preponderance of utility capital needs, the volume of external finance in future will be much greater. Applying the historically determined funding ratios to the estimated capital needs by industry yields a requirement of $750 billion that must be met from the world's capital markets. Before the budget, we thought it reasonable to suppose that domestic capital markets, institutions and banks would be likely to provide more than half of the total financing, some $400 to $450 billion, with the balance raised from outside Canada. By industry, the electrical sector, as expected, accounts for nearly $500 billion or nearly 70 per cent of the total. The petroleum and coal sectors require $172 billion while $87 billion represents the expected external financing by the pipeline and gas distribution industries.

Foreign borrowing

In an energy-hungry world in which all nations must diversify their energy supply industries, the solutions tend to be capital-intensive, and no nation will require more capital than the United States itself. At the same time, the United States will suffer the same current account problems as Canada does — because of its dependence on imported petroleum. Thus, we must suspect the ability of the U.S.A. to sustain large-scale capital exports. Looking ahead, in the case of Canada, cumulative offshore energy borrowing could reach $350 billion over the next 20 years. The electric utility industry is projected to require almost $200 billion from offshore capital markets while the petroleum and coal sectors will need over $100 billion. The remainder, some $50 billion will be needed for pipelines. In the context of escalating world capital needs, it can readily be seen that finding these massive sums in the world's capital markets will pose a formidable challenge.

Souring the climate

This country is going to need the maximum amount of domestic investment capital which can be generated plus very significant amounts of external capital to develop its energy potential. Suppressing the revenue flow to producers and imposing a significant new tax burden through the non-deductible imposition of an 8 per cent tax on gross revenue less operating costs will have a serious impact on the climate in which this capital must be raised.

First, industry's cash flow will not grow sufficiently to finance the enormous exploration and development expenses which are required to bring on additional supply. This will be particularly true in the first few years of the new Energy Program. If firms are unable to finance expansion internally, as they have done in the past, greater resort to external capital will be required. Capital which, as we have noted, will have many suitors as the decade advances. One source of capital, the long-term bond market, has proved very unpredictable in the past year and a half and it therefore seems likely that, increasingly, energy firms will need finance from banks.

Banks, however, will be constrained by the amount of exposure which they prudently can assume in the energy field. In any event, lower cash flows reduce the capacity of energy firms to service bank financing. The grant system for funding exploration and development activity will be helpful in mitigating the worst effects but to some extent these provisions merely replace the former depletion allowance arrangements.

A second factor impacting the future availability of capital is the fact that because of the new ownership provisions, the activity level of the major firms will be reduced. In the past, the majors have been important providers of equity capital in Canada. In part they will be replaced by small and medium-sized domestic firms who typically borrow more heavily. This will raise the already rising debt-equity ratio for the industry. As the degree of leverage rises, the cost of capital will escalate. In addition, the trend to more highly leveraged domestic firms will likely increase our reliance on foreign borrowing as long as the net supply of capital in Canada remains inadequate.

There is one avenue which remains open to improve what will otherwise be a dismal picture on the capital side that is that, following further negotiations with the producing provinces, the federal government might raise the wellhead price to the producer. Indeed, if Canada is to achieve crude oil self-sufficiency by the early 1990s, one of the NEP's goals, we strongly believe faster rates of increase in wellhead prices are required. This is particularly true of the first half of the 1980s when the projected cash flow of the industry will otherwise be depressed.

The impact on a typical project

The impact of the budget on cash flows and rate of return in the industry can best be seen by considering the actual circumstances of a hypothetical, but typical exploration project in Alberta. The case assumptions are set out in Table I and the results reported in Tables II and III. We should point out that the case has been constructed on the basis of oil prices that appear in the budget and assume that those

TABLE I
EFFECTS OF THE BUDGET PROPOSALS ON AN EXPLORATION PROJECT IN ALBERTA
Case Assumptions

1. Taxes:
   Revenue Tax of 8% is applied on gross revenues *before* royalties but after direct operating costs.

   Corporate tax is assumed to be 36% (federal) and 11% (Alberta).

2. Capital:
   In assuming an exploratory risk of 33%, it is implied that three trys must be made to obtain one success. Therefore, three exploration wells must be drilled and sufficient land for three wells must be obtained.

Investment Category	Investments M$ Risk Free	Risked
Land	640	1,920
Exploration Drilling	300	950*
Development Drilling	350	875**
Tie-In and Facilities, etc.	550	550

*Includes an extra $50M for the successful exploration well
**Development risk is 80%

   Investments are assumed to take place over 1981.

3. Production and Reserves:
   Three wells producing 200 BOPD in 1982, declining harmonically at 10% over a twenty-year life. Total reserves before royalty are 819 MBBLS.

4. Royalty:
   New oil in Alberta averaging 19%.

5. Operating Costs:
   $750 per well per month plus $2 per barrel.

6. Operating Inflation:

	1981	1982	1983	1984	1985	1986	Thereafter
%	10	10	9	8	7	6	6

TABLE II
EFFECTS OF THE BUDGET PROPOSALS ON AN EXPLORATION PROJECT IN ALBERTA NO PRICE CHANGE BEFORE TAX CASH FLOWS
$000's
(percentage change from pre-budget in brackets)

	1981	1982	1983	1984	1985	1986	1987	1988	1989	1990	Total
Case 1: Pre-Budget	4,295	872	915	914	915	939	961	946	935	946	4,048
		(-)	(-)	(-)	(-)	(-)	(-)	(-)	(-)	(-)	(-)
Case 2: Post-Budget	4,295	769	807	808	811	834	855	843	835	847	3,116
(No incentives)		(-12)	(-12)	(-12)	(-11)	(-11)	(-11)	(-11)	(-11)	(-10)	(-23)
Case 3: Post-Budget	4,113	769	807	808	811	834	855	843	835	847	3,299
(10% Incentives)		(-12)	(-12)	(-12)	(-11)	(-11)	(-11)	(-11)	(-11)	(-10)	(-19)
Case 4: Post-Budget	3,788	769	807	808	811	834	855	843	835	847	3,624
(35% Incentives)		(-12)	(-12)	(-12)	(-11)	(-11)	(-11)	(-11)	(-11)	(-10)	(-10)
Case 5: Post-Budget	3,788	769	807	808	811	834	855	843	835	847	3,624
(35% Incentives No explor. depl.)		(-12)	(-12)	(-12)	(-11)	(-11)	(-11)	(-11)	(-11)	(-10)	(-10)

TABLE III
EFFECTS OF THE BUDGET PROPOSALS ON AN EXPLORATION PROJECT IN ALBERTA
NO PRICE CHANGE AFTER TAX CASH FLOWS
$000's
(percentage change from pre-budget in brackets)

	1981	1982	1983	1984	1985	1986	1987	1988	1989	1990	Total
Case 1: Pre-Budget	4,295	872	915	857	688	581	580	563	552	558	1,871
		(-)	(-)	(-)	(-)	(-)	(-)	(-)	(-)	(-)	(-)
Case 2: Post-Budget	4,295	769	807	637	561	476	475	461	452	459	802
(No incentives)		(-12)	(-12)	(-26)	(-18)	(-18)	(-18)	(-18)	(-18)	(-18)	(-57)
Case 3: Post-Budget	4,113	769	786	596	479	473	472	459	451	458	832
(10% Incentives)		(-12)	(-14)	(-30)	(-30)	(-19)	(-19)	(-18)	(-18)	(-18)	(-56)
Case 4: Post-Budget	3,788	769	710	511	475	470	470	458	450	457	983
(35% Incentives)		(-12)	(-22)	(-40)	(-31)	(-19)	(-19)	(-19)	(-18)	(-18)	(-47)
Case 5: Post-Budget	3,788	769	669	495	475	470	470	458	450	457	925
(35% Incentives No explor. depl.)		(-12)	(-27)	(-42)	(-31)	(-19)	(-19)	(-19)	(-18)	(-18)	(-51)

prices had been correctly anticipated for the first five years. Prices beyond five years are not those included in the budget but are forecasts based on a more conservative set of assumptions. This latter option reflects Campbell Watkins' assessment elsewhere in this volume to the effect that since the period beyond five years exceeds the certain life of the present government there is no strong reason to expect that the proposed oil prices will be effectively obtained. We use the term "effectively obtained" to indicate the possibility that additional tax measures may reduce the effective producer price even if the Energy Program prices are obtained in the second half of the 1980s.

Looked at from the perspective of a potential financier of this energy project, the impact of the budget has obviously been quite severe. The after tax present worth of the project (Table IV) assuming a conventional 15 per cent discount rate, is reduced from $98,000 on a pre-budget basis to a negative valuation of $313,000 in the post-budget situation. This decline in value arises in the most generous incentives case and is only about half the potential devaluation in cases where no incentives are acquired.

As the cash flows presented in Tables II and III clearly show, much of the damage is done in the first five years of the program. During 1982, the first year of the hypothetical undertaking, the project would realize a minimum after tax cash flow reduction of 12 per cent. Over the period to 1990 the reduction amounts to a minimum of 47 per cent. If no incentives were obtained the total loss could be as high as 57 per cent over the period. There can be no ambiguity as to the effect such changed circumstances would have on this hypothetical firm's access to capital.

The effect on gas producers

The outlook for gas producers appears to us to be even more dismal. Not only do they face a frozen wellhead price next year, weak export demand and a backing-up of the 30¢ export tax onto their net-backs but they must also bear the heavy effect of the net revenue tax and the weight of future increases in transportation charges to the East. Certainly, none of these factors can provide much encouragement to gas producers. Fortunately, the Alberta government's decision to impose production cutbacks does not extend to natural gas and eventually, according to our simulations, cash flows to gas producers will improve markedly due to future acceleration of the wellhead price. However, this relief is a half decade away and extends beyond the term of the existing government.

TABLE IV
EFFECTS OF THE BUDGET PROPOSALS ON AN EXPLORATION PROJECT IN ALBERTA NO PRICE CHANGE

	Rate of Return %		Payout, Years		Present Worth $000's	
	BTAX	ATAX	BTAX	ATAX	15% Discount BTAX	ATAX
Case 1: Pre-Budget	21.2	15.5	5.7	6.7	1,507	98
Case 2: Post-Budget (No Incentives)	18.8	12.0	6.3	8.2	904	-588
Case 3: Post-Budget (10% Incentives)	19.7	12.3	6.1	8.2	1,074	-505
Case 4: Post-Budget (35% Incentives)	21.4	13.3	5.7	7.8	1,377	-313
Case 5: Post-Budget (35% Incentives No explor. depl.)	21.4	13.0	5.7	8.0	1,377	-353

Note: BTAX is before tax cash flows
ATAX is after tax cash flows.

Regarding the Natural Gas Bank, we are not very encouraged by a program whereby the state taxes the gross revenue of resource firms in order to finance the purchase of a resource which it intends to store in the ground. The basic problem here is that the country faces a supply over-capacity in natural gas. One solution is precisely what the NEP aims to achieve, namely a high degree of inter-fuel substitution. Another solution would be to work toward an export pricing formula more attuned to market conditions in the United States. The NEP does not address this. Indeed, if the export tax is to result in further price increases there could be further price resistance by U.S. buyers and Canada may indeed be in danger of becoming merely a "surge tank" for American demand as Mr. John McNicholas of Petro-Canada suggested in the Fall of 1980.

Synthetic oil vs. conventional oil

The budget does provide substantial incentives for heavy oil upgrading and synthetic and frontier oil production. These are laudable measures which deserve wide and full recognition. In this context, we hope an early accommodation between Ottawa and Edmonton can be achieved whereby the Alsands and Cold Lake projects can proceed, although at the end of 1980 prospects look quite dim.

Far less generous incentives are provided for conventional oil and gas production from the established fields of Western Canada. The effect of this measure is that the country will be encouraging production of high cost frontier reserves and not fully exploiting the low cost reserves of the Western Sedimentary Basin. Given the oil price regime adopted, only a certain amount of capital can be raised by the energy sector and given allocation of it to longer term sources of supply will mean that total oil production in Canada in the 1980s will be less than in the case where more rapid exploitation of low-cost reserves occurred. Encouragement of frontier exploration is important in order to delineate more accurately the total reserves of the country. But we do not believe frontier development should take precedence over continued exploration and development of our lower-cost conventional reserves. The task of providing adequate incentive to producers in conventional areas, we might add, is the responsibility of both the federal and provincial governments.†

†Editor's Note: For additional comment on the implications of this shared responsibility see the essays by Ken Norrie and Tom Courchene in this volume.

B. CANADIANIZATION

Another controversial area of our new energy policy concerns the federal government's Canadianization program. At present, roughly 75 per cent of our oil and gas industry is owned by non-residents, principally by Americans.† Many in this country are of the opinion that such a strategic sector should be brought under greater domestic control. The NEP aims to have at least 50 per cent of the industry owned by Canadians by 1990 and to achieve this objective, several quite specific measures have been proposed. These include at least 50 per cent Canadian control of frontier oil developments and a grant system heavily weighted towards domestic firms. If implemented, we believe the 50 per cent target will be achieved much earlier than 1990, possibly before 1985.

The measures announced are strong and will reduce the net worth and growth capacity of non-Canadian firms. The first evidence of this was the precipitous decline in the share value of foreign controlled firms in the three weeks following the budget. Canadian firms as a consequence will have improved opportunities but due to their leaner cash flow positions, it is unclear whether they will have the capacity to recreate the same degree of dynamism which formerly prevailed in the industry. A further point worth noting on this matter is that foreign controlled firms do not "control" energy resources in Canada in the sense that they can do as they wish. Both provincial and federal governments have quite extensive control over energy firms and their activities — indeed recently this control has been growing very rapidly. However, it is true that foreign firms do obtain the bulk of the profits accruing from the production and sale of this country's oil and gas. To the extent that windfall profits were being earned and repatriated, there can be quite legitimate concern here.

The new fiscal regime will ensure that major windfall gains are not being repatriated. However, it may also ensure that non-resident firms play a less active and constructive role in Canadian energy development. There are many energy hotspots in this world and investment capital tends to be quite mobile. Canada, with its enviable record of political and economic stability and large resource endowment has many advantages but these could be quickly negated by imprudent energy pricing and unduly nationalistic actions. We in the financial

†Editor's Note: The 75 per cent ownership figure is subject to further discussion in the paper by M. Walker in this volume.

community have a very significant interest in a healthy vibrant Canadian energy industry and we are confident that domestic firms will thrive and play an increasingly large part in these energy developments. But, we also believe there is an important role in Canada for foreign firms who are active, constructive energy developers.

We might add that we are in agreement with some recent comments by Mr. Geoffrey Stevens regarding the proposed treatment of multinational firms operating in Canada. It is unwise, and we believe ultimately detrimental, for Canada, on the one hand, to become a signatory to an OECD declaration granting equal treatment to both domestic and foreign firms while, with the other hand, introducing clearly discriminatory energy provisions. Part of the problem was that most government incentives in the oil and gas field formerly were provided through tax incentives which particularly benefited large taxable and principally foreign firms. The move to grants which will benefit all firms including smaller Canadian companies should be welcomed. The step beyond that to grants which discriminate on the basis of nationality are quite unwise. Canada is a small, open and internationally-oriented country which should be in the vanguard of non-discrimination partly because we have so much to lose in fields such as foreign trade, overseas investments by Canadian multinationals and banking.

III. BEYOND THE BUDGET

There are three broad issues which we should like also to raise, namely the role which the energy sector might play in the overall economy, secondly, the issue of using energy revenue to finance general government activity and thirdly, the establishment of stable and fair rules of the game.

A. THE ENERGY SECTOR AS A GROWTH POLE

The massive energy investment program which might occur in Canada implies a doubling of the energy investment share in the country's GNP. Clearly there is the potential in the energy sector to provide the impetus and the dynamism for a major Canadian economic expansion. Total energy reserves are widely dispersed throughout Canada and all regions would benefit from the propulsion out of the current low and stagnating level of economic activity to near full employment of our labour and capital resources. The industrial manufacturing heartland of Southern Ontario and Quebec would benefit directly in terms of supplying materials and services to energy projects and indirectly through the higher aggregate level of economic activity. To some extent, this activity in the form of Canadian imports would spill over onto our trading partners, and as was earlier mentioned, our most significant international contribution could be increased energy exports to our energy-short trading partners and allies. These are powerful reasons for harnessing our energy potential.

B. ENERGY REVENUES AND GOVERNMENT DEFICITS

The second issue pertains to the use of energy revenues collected by governments to finance deficits. By the quirk of geology, much of the oil and gas is located in Alberta. Consequently, Alberta, a province of two million, is disproportionately wealthy with government surplus accounts totalling over $10 billion. Conversely, the federal government is running a $14 billion deficit.† Because of the large deficit, the federal government has precious little room for expansionary economic measures or programs which it might wish to introduce.

To reduce the deficit, the federal government has identified the energy sector as the most lucrative portion of the economy to raise large additional amounts of revenue. However, in the longer run, surely taxing the revenue stream which is flowing into productive, necessary investment and diverting the revenue stream to pay for a government deficit comprised largely of operating expenses, that is consumption activity, is unwise. Reducing the federal deficit, which is a very worthwhile objective in itself, can best be achieved, in our opinion, by stringent expenditure control designed to reduce non-essential government spending and by resort to broadly based taxes which principally curb consumption spending. With the anticipated massive energy investment requirements, Canada needs to constrain consumption and direct resources into investment activity. Funding government deficits from energy revenue surely will not achieve this objective.

†Editor's Note: For more on the appropriate division of energy revenues, see the papers by Norrie and Courchene in this volume.

C. THE CHANGING FACE OF ENERGY POLICY

Our third point is that in recent years the most distinguishing characteristic, and we are using the word "distinguishing" in the sense of being typical or of identifying traits in energy policy and not in the sense of being distinguished or commendable, has been the numerous times energy policy has been altered. In fairness to energy policy-makers, the world of the 1970s and 1980s was and is a volatile place, where some degree of policy change is both necessary and desirable. This issue is largely a matter of degree and we firmly believe the need in the 1980s, in the face of the unprecedented energy investments which must be made in North America, is for greater policy stability.

The rules of this game must be more certain and dependable if investors and energy producers are to get on with the essential job of producing energy. Foremost in terms of policy stability in Canada is an expeditious settlement of the inter-governmental dispute through an understanding of what constitutes a fair share, for the federal and provincial governments and for producers, of rising energy prices. There can be little question that the current energy dispute is seriously detrimental to the longer-term interests of all the parties involved. Establishing the rules of the game and ensuring producers adequate returns are the two primary prerequisites for accelerated exploration and development in this country. These are the first priorities in Canada for the achievement of our energy potential.

The importance of seeming stable

The scale of prospective energy investment in Canada is so large that extensive resort to international capital markets will be required. Industrial restructuring and massive energy investments in the U.S.A. will strain American capital markets and reverse the long-standing history of net capital exports from that country to Canada. Globally, capital markets will be tight and Canada will need to convince capital investors that the investment climate here is fair and stable. The retroactive back-in provisions granted to Petro-Canada already are creating international shock waves. Additionally, prospective tar sands' investors might quite legitimately wonder if one day they will be "Suncored", that is where overnight their wellhead price will tumble by 56 per cent.

Frankly, we agree with many of the more controversial objectives of the NEP — of increasing Canadian ownership and increasing the federal government's revenue share, but the means of achieving these objectives appear precipitous and without full consideration of the impact on the longer-term investment climate. The issues of changing the rules of the game and substantially increasing state intrusion transcend the energy sector. These are important issues for the long-run vigour of the Canadian economy as a whole and are deserving of greater discussion.

The energy challenge in this country is very great indeed. The budget and the NEP will, we are certain, lead to a significant increase in the level of Canadian ownership. Whether an expansion of total exploration and development and, as a consequence, self-sufficiency occurs is far more questionable unless some of the provisions of the NEP are changed.

Chapter 3

Mr. Lalonde and the Price Mechanism: or Never the Twain Shall Meet

G.C. WATKINS

DataMetrics Limited and University of Calgary

THE AUTHOR

GORDON CAMPBELL WATKINS, born in Cheshire, England in 1939, is President of the economic consulting firm of DataMetrics, Calgary, and is also Visiting Professor of Economics at the University of Calgary. He graduated from Leeds University, Honours B.A. Economics and Statistics, 1960; took degree courses in accountancy at Manchester University, 1961; and received his M.Phil., 1972, from Leeds University.

After two years as statistician with an English engineering firm, Professor Watkins came to Canada, and from 1962 to 1972 he served as an economist with several government agencies and corporations. He joined DataMetrics as President in 1973. Professor Watkins' involvement in economic research spans a wide range of projects and positions: Chief Economist at the Oil and Gas Conservation Board (1965-1969); Associate Economist, Royal Bank of Canada (1970-1971); Director of Economic Studies — Gas Arctic Group (1971-1972). As well as his involvement in petroleum research, Professor Watkins has also directed and participated in studies related to road transport, aviation, cost-benefit analyses and regional economic impact studies.

Professor Watkins has published papers in a wide range of professional and academic journals, including the *Canadian Journal of Economics*, *Journal of Industrial Economics*, *Journal of Environmental Economics and Management*, *Journal of Finance*, *Journal of Business Administration*, *The Journal of Canadian Petroleum Technology*, and such trade journals as *Oilweek* and *Canadian Petroleum*. He was Co-editor of *Oil in the Seventies*: *Essays on Energy Policy* (1977, with Michael A. Walker).

Mr. Lalonde and the Price Mechanism: or Never the Twain Shall Meet

G.C. WATKINS
DataMetrics Limited
*and University of Calgary**

I. INTRODUCTION

The energy strategy of the Canadian government in 1976 called for moving "domestic oil prices towards international levels"[1], but this is not what happened. In 1976, domestic prices were about 70 per cent of world prices at Montreal; in November 1980 the corresponding figure is about 50 per cent.[2] In this sense, then, the policies outlined in the National Energy Program (NEP)[3] which seek to 'disassociate' Canadian oil from world price levels do not represent a new departure, since the 1976 intentions were not consummated. In fact, the new policy is consistent with, and an extension of, the drift over the past few years of a widening gap between Canadian and world oil prices.

In what follows below, first the oil and gas pricing proposals in the NEP are summarized. The discussion of them proceeds by reviewing the perceptions of the world oil market which emerge from the NEP and have an important bearing on the domestic price policies put forward. Then certain economic efficiency aspects of the NEP oil pricing regime are outlined, distinguishing between demand and supply side effects. The next section concerns natural gas prices. Some concluding remarks summarize the paper.

*Helpful comments were made by John Rowse of the University of Calgary; the usual disclaimer applies. I am indebted to research assistance from Roger Lawrey of DataMetrics Limited.

II. WHAT ARE THE DOMESTIC OIL AND GAS PRICING PROPOSALS IN THE NATIONAL ENERGY PROGRAM?

The main burden of the pricing provisions for the NEP relate to oil. A 'blended' oil pricing regime is to be introduced. It bears some similarity to the discredited and now discarded oil pricing policy of the United States.

The proposed blended price system is intented to fold the costs of different sources of oil into one weighted average price to consumers across Canada. Three types of domestic oil are recognized: conventional, synthetic and tertiary. The prices for each domestic category are to be set as follows:

1. *Conventional Oil*

   From January 1, 1981, for a period of three years the wellhead price of conventional oil will increase by $1.00 per barrel every six months. This increase will be raised to $2.25 every six months until the end of 1985. Consequently, by the end of 1983 wellhead prices will be $22.75 per barrel; by the end of 1985 they will be $31.75 per barrel.

2. *Synthetic Crude Oil*

   The reference price for synthetic oil from the oil sands for January 1, 1981, is set at the lesser of $38.00 per barrel or the world price. This reference price will be escalated thereafter by the lesser of the Consumer Price Index (CPI) or the world price.

3. *Tertiary Enhanced Recovery Oil*

   The NEP provides for a 'tertiary supplement' to be paid to qualifying producers of enhanced recovery oil. This supplement will make the total wellhead price of oil recovered through tertiary recovery methods on January 1, 1981, approximately $30.00 per barrel.[4] The tertiary reference price will be adjusted annually in a manner similar to the synthetic oil reference price. This incentive will only be offered in "provinces that maintain or, preferably, enrich existing fiscal incentives for tertiary production."[5]

Incentives for upgrading of heavy crude oil and production of specified frontier oil may be established when more detailed information on costs and timing of production is available. Thus, more categories could be created to which special price provisions would apply.

The NEP oil pricing proposals at the wellhead are summarized in Table I below. The table extends to 1985. The NEP shows numbers which extend to 1990. For example, conventional oil prices are projected to more than double, 1985 to 1990, a higher rate of increase than in the near term. Although these intentions are no doubt well meant, they extend beyond the life of the current government and given a previous lack of correspondence between intentions and reality (see Introduction), they cannot but be seen as lacking in credibility.

TABLE I
NATIONAL ENERGY PROGRAM: WELLHEAD OIL PRICES
($/bbl)

	Oil Sands Reference Price	Tertiary Recovery Oil (15° API Gravity)	Conventional Oil (38° API Gravity)
January 1980	—	—	14.75
August 1980	—	—	16.75
January 1981	38.00	30.00	17.75
July 1981			18.75
January 1982	41.85	33.05	19.75
July 1982			20.75
January 1983	45.80	36.15	21.75
July 1983			22.75
January 1984	49.85	39.35	25.00
July 1984			27.25
January 1985	54.10	42.70	29.50
July 1985			31.75

Source: NEP, p. 26.

The blended oil price system

The blended price consumers face will eventually include the full cost of oil imports. This addition to the weighted average price of the three domestic supply categories will be phased in as follows. In December

1980, refiners will pay a new Petroleum Compensation Charge (PCC), which incorporates the Syncrude levy paid to existing oil sands plants. This charge will be $2.55 per barrel, comprising $1.75 for Syncrude and $0.80 to cover a portion of oil import compensation costs. The PCC will increase by $2.50 per barrel on January 1, 1981, 1982 and 1983. The full cost of imports will be absorbed in the blended price by 1984. The eventual blended price will never exceed 85 per cent of the international price of oil or the average U.S. price, whichever is lower.

On this basis, the refinery gate price of conventional oil would reach $32.80 per barrel by the end of 1983 and $41.80 per barrel by the end of 1985, from an August 1980 figure of $18.50.

This outline of the NEP pricing provisions does not include allowance for the proposed levy on oil and gas consumption to be devoted to the takeover of foreign-owned oil companies, the so-called foreign ownership charge (OC).[6] Such an allowance, of course, is only notional at this time. It will not directly affect the supply side economic efficiency calculations made subsequently in this paper, since it simply represents a transfer from oil and gas consumers to foreign shareholders, via a conduit such as Petro-Canada Limited. However, to the degree imposed it does have implications for the 'demand side' calculations discussed below.

Natural gas prices

In recent years, the wellhead price of natural gas has increased at Toronto by about $0.15 per Mcf for every $1.00 per barrel increase in the wellhead price of oil. In 1981, the Eastern Canada city-gate price is to remain at its current level in order to accommodate a new federal tax on natural gas of $0.30 per Mcf. For 1982 and 1983, city-gate prices inclusive of the export tax are scheduled to increase by $0.45 per Mcf, of which $0.15 per Mcf would represent a rise in the export tax. Wellhead prices for gas are not shown in the NEP, but if a representative set of gas pipeline tariffs are deducted from the Eastern Canada city-gate prices — assumed to be Toronto — the Alberta border gas prices shown in Table II are derived. In Eastern Canada, the ratio of natural gas prices to oil prices will fall over time, 80 per cent in 1980 to 67 per cent in November 1983. No indication of natural gas prices following 1983 is given in the NEP.

The federal government indicates an inflation rate of some 10.5 per cent for 1981; double-digit inflation may well extend to 1984-85. Table III expresses the NEP price proposals in real (inflation adjusted) as well as nominal terms, given a 10 per cent inflation rate beyond 1981. The nominal prices represent annual averages. Unfortunately, a 10 per cent inflation rate may prove conservative.

These figures show wellhead prices for conventional oil increasing modestly in real terms, at an annual average rate of 3.3 per cent, 1981 to 1985. The rise in consumer prices for oil at the refinery gate — given the blended price system — shows an increase in real terms at an annual average rate of 4.4 per cent, 1981 to 1985.

III. THE INTERNATIONAL OIL MARKET: A CAPRICIOUS ARTIFICIALITY?

The NEP's view of world oil prices emerges at various points in the text, but can be represented by this quotation:

> "World oil prices are arbitrary and artificial. They do not reflect conditions of competitive supply and demand nor the cost of production in Canada or other countries."[7]

Elsewhere in the NEP, several references are made to the instability, political sensitivity, chaos, uncertainty and erratic nature of world oil prices.[8]

The argument that world oil prices do not reflect the cost of production in Canada or other countries is fallacious. If substantial volumes of oil production were available from non-OPEC countries at costs significantly below OPEC prices, and if such sources were willing to produce, then the resultant pressures on the world oil market would be manifest. Yet this is not what has happened. It follows that either non-OPEC supplies at OPEC prices are not abundant, or countries with them prefer to let them languish. What does not follow is that OPEC prices are somehow created in a vacuum, without any relation to the costs and availability of other supplies. Clearly, the latter is an important limitation on the scope for OPEC to raise prices.

The more crucial part of the preceding quote from the NEP is the view that world oil prices are "arbitrary and artificial". Arbitrary means derived from mere opinion or random choice, unrestrained. Artificial means not natural. Neither term is correct as a description of world oil prices as, for example, developments over the past two years can illustrate.

In 1979, the Iranian imbroglio took about 5 million barrels a day of oil off the world market, about 15 per cent of total OPEC production.

TABLE II
NATURAL GAS PRICES AND TAXES
($/Mcf)

	Domestic Alberta Border Price (1)	TCPL Tariff Alberta Border/ Toronto (2)	Eastern Canada City-Gate Price (3)	Cumulative Natural Gas Tax (4)	Total (5)
Oct. 31, 1980	1.93	0.67	2.60	—	2.60
Nov. 1, 1980	1.93	0.67	2.60	0.30	2.90
July 1, 1981	1.86	0.74	2.60	0.45	3.05
Jan. 1, 1982	1.69	0.91	2.60	0.60	3.20
Feb. 1, 1982	1.84	0.91	2.75	0.60	3.35
Aug. 1, 1982	1.99	0.91	2.90	0.60	3.50
Jan. 1, 1983	1.83	1.07	2.90	0.75	3.65
Feb. 1, 1983	1.98	1.07	3.05	0.75	3.80
Aug. 1, 1983	2.13	1.07	3.20	0.75	3.95

Sources: (1) = (3) – (2)
(2) DataMetrics Limited
(3) NEP, page 35
(4) NEP, page 35
(5) = (3) + (4)

TABLE III
PRICE PROPOSALS IN NOMINAL AND REAL TERMS: ANNUAL AVERAGES

	(1) Wellhead Conventional Oil Prices		(2) Conventional Blended Oil Prices		(3) Alberta Border Natural Gas Prices		(4) City Gate Natural Gas Prices	
	nominal $/bbls	real	nominal $/bbls	real	nominal $/Mcf	real	nominal $/Mcf	real
1981	18.25	18.25	23.80	23.80	1.90	1.90	2.98	2.98
1982	20.25	18.33	27.80	25.16	1.89	1.71	3.39	3.07
1983	22.25	18.31	32.80	26.57	2.03	1.67	3.84	3.16
1984	26.13	19.54	36.18	27.06				
1985	30.63	20.83	40.68	27.66	not projected beyond 1983			

Source: (1) NEP, page 26
(2) NEP, page 26
(3) See Table II
(4) NEP, page 32

Spot world crude markets responded quickly. The jump in spot prices dragged up the whole OPEC price structure. The question of whether buyers over-reacted in panic may be left aside. The fact remains there was a perceived shortage of oil. Lo and behold, prices rose. The substantial degree of increase reflected the reality of a lack of alternative supplies and relatively inelastic demand and supply price elasticities in the short run. That is, there was scope for prices to rise without significant countervailing demand and supply responses, especially in the short term.

By the summer of 1980, before the Iran-Iraq conflagration, the situation was quite different. Spot markets were soft. Demand for OPEC oil had receded, and the OPEC pricing structure was under downward pressure. Previously mooted price increases were withheld. Saudi Arabia was taking the opportunity to use its production leverage to impose a more cohesive OPEC pricing structure at levels aligned to the lower Saudi Arabian prices.

The precise details of the world oil pricing situation need not detain us, nor the emergence of tighter market conditions with the virtual elimination of exports from Iraq. The point is that world oil prices are not capricious — an arbitrary whim. Neither are they artificial, unrelated to any natural elements. Instead, they are grounded in the complex realities of demand and supply responses, the weighing of opportunities by the main producers for production now rather than later, the impact of production dislocations, absorptive capacity of OPEC countries, rates of return on financial assets and the like. Certainly world oil prices can be unstable and sensitive to political events — this is what the market registers — but such responses are far from arbitrary.

The world oil market does not approximate the economist's cherished ideal of perfect competition — a multitude of sellers confronting a multitude of buyers, none of which can individually affect the price by their own actions. Consequently, the pattern of prices established in the world oil market does not correspond to that in a fully competitive market, and to this extent the NEP supposition that world oil prices do not reflect 'conditions of competitive supply and demand' is correct. But there also is the presumption underlying the NEP that rising prices on world oil markets are 'artificial', to use the NEP's term.

Nearly 50 years ago, in a classic statement of the problem, Harold Hotelling showed that in competitive markets the price of a resource produced from a fixed stock should rise at a rate equal to the rate of interest to ensure the optimal use of the resource.[9] Recently, the actions of OPEC have rekindled speculation in optimal or 'best' price patterns for production of stock type resources over time. In these exercises, the various assumptions implicit in the classical approach have been relaxed. Stocks (reserves) are not fixed and immutable. Producers may have different interests; they may be "savers" or "spenders". 'Backstop' technologies may be assumed, where at a certain price substantial volumes of alternative forms of energy become available. Several models have been constructed to investigate in this sort of context what appear to be optimal price trajectories over time, where various criteria are used to define what is being optimized.[10]

One result most of these models have in common is the prediction of a rising trajectory of real world oil prices over time. That is, they predict oil prices will continue to rise faster than the overall rate of inflation. This fundamental outcome is quite insensitive to what criterion is adopted as a maximand and some of the models produce prices not out of line with current world oil price levels. While few of these models attempt to simulate what a truly competitive market would yield, the mere fact that such models can generate price patterns consistent with OPEC pricing trends means the general pattern of OPEC prices over time cannot be termed 'arbitrary and artificial'.

The characterization of the world oil market in such terms in the NEP is unfortunate, because it tends to distract attention from the realities which the world oil market expresses, and induces an ostrich-like attitude toward domestic pricing. This much is apparent in the NEP statement:

> "Clearly any country able to dissociate itself from the world oil market in 1980 should do so and quickly."[11]

For an energy-rich or potentially energy-rich country such as Canada, this admonition is by no means clear. Given abundant *potential* energy resources in Canada,[12] world oil prices can represent an opportunity, rather than a debilitating frustration. In other words, world oil prices provide scope for the energy industry to become a productive growth 'pole', a situation we can exploit rather than attempt to suppress. Moreover, and as is implicit in the following discussion of demand and supply responses, paradoxically, dissociation from the world oil market may well tend to increase reliance on it.

IV. BLENDED OIL PRICING: DEMAND SIDE INEFFICIENCIES

Canadian domestic oil production is at capacity now, and will remain so over the next few years — especially if Premier Lougheed compresses Alberta capacity by government fiat. At any rate, given domestic capacity constraints, the marginal source of oil consumption in Canada is imported oil or diversion of domestic oil from export markets. This will still hold in the Orwellian year 1984, the year when the total costs of oil imports are transferred directly to oil consumers via the Petroleum Compensation Charge. Even the most optimistic advocates of the NEP probably do not expect domestic capacity to be in surplus and oil imports to have been extinguished by then. In fact, more sober analysis[13] suggests the degree of Canadian dependence on imports may have increased.

Canadian evidence on oil demand supports the economist's law of downward sloping demand; as prices fall, consumers buy more; as prices rise, they buy less. What is not known is the precise degree of response of consumer demand to price variations. Empirical studies have thrown up quite a wide range of estimates. A representative estimate adopted here of the price elasticity of demand for petroleum production is -0.5. This is intended to represent a long-run response.[14] The price elasticity says that when the real price of petroleum rises (falls) by 10 per cent, demand eventually falls (rises) by 5 per cent — all other factors affecting energy demand held constant.

In this section we provide estimates of the economic inefficiencies, in terms of oil demand, that will be engendered when the blended oil pricing regime is fully implemented in 1984.† Given the number of assumptions required for these estimates, the results can only be indicative of the order of magnitude of the sums involved. In the interest of providing conservative estimates, the calculations assume no increase in world oil prices in *real* terms beyond current (December 1980) levels; these levels include allowance for the December OPEC increases. Recent history and the economic modelling discussed above suggest this assumption is optimistic.

Given the provisions of the NEP and assuming no increase in real world oil prices, the spread between world oil prices and the domestic blended price will be about $23 per barrel by 1984. Total consumption

†Editor's Note: Readers interested in the methodology used to calculate these estimates should contact the author or the Fraser Institute for a copy of the technical memorandum which describes the procedure.

of oil in Canada is projected to be about 650 million barrels per year. The price elasticity of –0.5 suggests 108 million barrels or 16.6 per cent of such consumption will have been stimulated by the policy of holding domestic prices below world levels to this degree.[15] Since the marginal source to satisfy such incremental demand is imported oil (or diverted exports), this higher consumption will cost the Canadian economy an estimated $8.1 billion — the product of the volume of additional consumption and the price of world oil. Consumer benefits from this additional consumption are estimated as the amount they pay at the lower domestic price plus the associated 'consumer surplus' — the excess of the amount consumers would be willing to pay to consume the extra amount of oil, over what they have to pay. In combination these two elements are estimated as $6.9 billion.

The difference between the costs and benefits is a net cost of $1.2 billion per year. It represents the estimated net economic loss on the additional consumption of oil eventually stimulated by holding domestic 'blended' prices below world prices to the extent they would be in 1984, as long as world oil prices in real terms do not rise further from 1980 levels. This is a deadweight loss to the economy, one not offset by gains elsewhere: the Gross National Product will be lower by $1.2 billion. Details of the calculation are shown in Table IV.

This efficiency loss is not the only one attributal to blended oil pricing. The scheme itself devolves substantial administrative costs on both government and industry; increased reliance on foreign oil compared with the lesser reliance if prices were aligned more closely to world prices entails security of supply costs. Moreover, price controls tend to preclude economic adjustments signified by changing world oil markets and, hence, lead to a deterioration in the ability of the economy to accommodate shocks from these and other sources. The cost of this inflexibility is very real, even if difficult to ascertain.

One virtue of the blended price system is that the full cost of oil imports is included in the average price of oil products, instead of being subsidized out of general tax revenue, as occurs at present. Under this current system there is little or no correlation between the price paid for imports and domestic prices. At least, the blended price system will restore a degree of correlation, albeit not to the extent suggested by economic efficiency objectives.

TABLE IV
AN ESTIMATE OF OIL DEMAND EFFICIENCY LOSSES
BLENDED OIL PRICING REGIME, 1984
(all $ figures are $ Canadian)

1.[1]	Oil consumption of which	650 MM bbls/year
	1a imported oil	220 MM bbls/year
	1b old oil	325 MM bbls/year
	1c synthetic	65 MM bbls/year
	1d tertiary	40 MM bbls/year
2.[2]	Representative domestic product oil price Toronto	$52.50 per bbl
3.	Cost of 1984 oil consumption at domestic prices = (1 × 2)	$34,125 million/year
4.[3]	Representative world oil product price, Toronto	$75.40 per bbl
5.	Implicit per barrel subsidy (4 – 2)	$22.90 per bbl
6.	Implicit subsidy on current oil consumption = (5 × 1)	$14,885 million/year
7.	Estimated consumption at world price	542 MM bbls/year
8.[4]	Estimated additional consumption at domestic price = (1 – 7)	108 MM bbls/year
9.	Implicit cost of additional consumption at domestic prices = (8 × 4)	$8,143 million/year
10.	Implicit benefit of additional consumption at domestic price, of which	$6,907 million/year
	10a benefit at domestic price = (8 × 2)	$5,670 million/year
	10b[5] consumer surplus = ½ (5 × 8)	$1,237 million/year
11.	Efficiency cost = (9 – 10)	$1,236 million/year

Notes:
1. Various forecasts.
2. Comprises weighted average price of Alberta crude plus gathering costs to Edmonton and IPL tariff to Toronto, plus Petroleum Compensation Charge, plus petroleum product taxes, plus distribution and refinery margins.
3. World crude oil price Toronto plus petroleum product taxes plus estimated distribution and refinery margins.
4. Assumes long run price elasticity of demand of –0.5.
5. Assumes linear demand curve over this interval.

V. SUPPLY INEFFICIENCIES UNDER BLENDED PRICES: THE GOVERNMENT AS MONOPSONIST

The National Energy Program says:

> "World prices or prices that are linked to world prices are not necessary to encourage increases in supply. . . . A price mechanism reflecting Canadian costs not international oil prices, and which offers high and predictable returns for higher cost and risky sources, is a better way to provide the necessary incentive."[16]

In ideal circumstances, what this view envisages is a government endowed with enough wisdom and information to be able to set prices for each component of supply at levels sufficient, but no more than sufficient, to entice the supply onto the market. 'Windfall' profits — which are taxable — are anathema:

> "It is not necessary to give producers windfall gains on these reserves in order to encourage new discoveries".[17]

One way of avoiding companies enjoying windfall profits is to select and set prices so that the exact correct quantities are picked off the "supply curve". The economist's supply curve is simply an array of supply sources arranged in order of increasing cost. Thus, it is upward sloping: more is supplied, the higher the price. At any one point in time, the Canadian oil supply curve might be illustrated in a simplified way, as shown in Figure 1.

With a competitive market, oil prices in Canada would be set by the world oil price; OM would be supplied at price P_w. Economic rent generated at world prices would be represented by the shaded area in Figure 1. This is the surplus over and above the price necessary to make the supply economic to produce. Varying proportions of this rent will accrue to governments, according to the severity of the tax and royalty system.

The intention of the NEP is to be able to pick supply off the supply curve by employing three sets of prices, as indicated in Figure 1. Some rent will be left with producers and will accrue to governments in their role as resource owners or taxing authorities. The resulting domestic output is to be sold at the blended price. There is a transfer from the producing sector and governments as resource owners to oil consumers and other levels of government.

If producer prices could be accurately administered by employing a sufficient number of differential prices, no overall economic inefficiency on the supply side would be perpetrated. To be sure, provincial governments as resource owners would grumble, and rightfully so. They would be faced with what is tantamount to a monopoly buyer, and would lose their share of economic rents.† But this would simply be a transfer between parties and would not involve any net national economic loss on the supply side (excluding administrative costs).

FIGURE 1
CANADIAN OIL SUPPLY

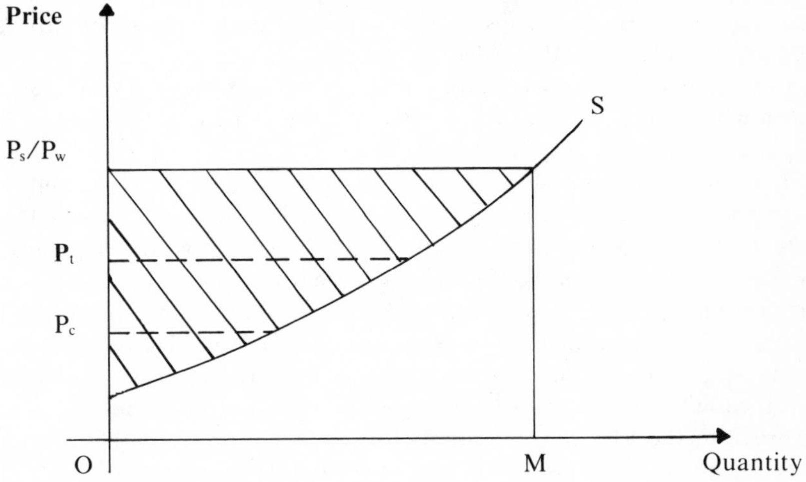

where P_c is the price of conventional oil
P_t is the price of tertiary oil
P_s is the price of synthetic oil
P_w is the world price of oil

The problem is that it is not possible to segregate supply with just three sets of prices in the way envisaged and avoid economic losses. Prices cannot be sufficiently 'fine tuned' to perform this function accurately. Recovery of oil from 'old' reservoirs will be curtailed over what would be recovered at prices more closely aligned to world levels. While incentives are offered for tertiary recovery, secondary recovery is ignored and as a result, production from secondary sources will be retarded. To the extent these kinds of resource losses are generated, they are irrevocable.

†Editor's Note: For more discussion of the governmental shares issue, see the essays by Professors Courchene and Norrie in this volume.

In contrast, the lack of incentive for new conventional oil from new discoveries does not necessarily mean an absolute resource loss. Rather, it may mean a deferral in discovery and development until such time these sources become economic. The timing of exploitation, then, may be somewhat less than optimal — higher cost sources may well be developed before those of lower cost — but the resources would not be extinguished. However, deferral of this happy day may be indefinite if oil prices do not keep pace with inflation. Since the price schedule to 1985 (see Table III) envisages only a modest increase in producer prices in real terms, in effect the potential for new conventional oil tends to be discarded by the NEP.

Estimates of supply side inefficiencies are made below.† Again, the caution that such estimates can only be of an order of magnitude applies.

The degree of response of oil supply to price variations is not well established. An inelastic response of 0.3 over the long run is assumed here for those categories of oil affected.[18] In other words, a price increase of 10 per cent would *eventually* yield increased domestic oil production of 3 per cent. Such additional production would be available for displacement of imported oil or for export. The degree of elasticity assumed is lower than figures more often used of around 0.5; the lower response of 0.3 is intended to allow for the higher prices awarded by the NEP to some supply sources, for example synthetic, to pick up much of the supply response relative to world prices.

The benefits on additional production of 134 million barrels estimated as forthcoming in response to world prices, valued at the equivalent world price, are calculated as $8.5 billion. The associated costs are estimated as $6.3 billion. The foregone net benefits, then, are estimated as $2.2 billion. This is a deadweight loss to the economy; Gross Domestic Product (GDP) is lower by this amount. Domestic oil costing less than the $63 per barrel we may pay for foreign oil in 1984 (but more than the domestic price) is not developed. Details of the calculation are shown in Table V.

A distributional adjustment is required to reflect foreign ownership. Recent analysis suggests[19] that in 1980 about 15 cents of every $1 increase in the price of oil accrues to foreign interests. Various aspects of the NEP might reduce this to, say, 10 cents on the dollar by 1984.

†Editor's Note: Readers interested in the methodology used to calculate these estimates should contact the author or the Fraser Institute for a copy of the technical memorandum which describes the procedure.

Accordingly, the supply side efficiency losses experienced could be substantially offset by virtue of the fact that at least some of the loss is visited upon foreigners. But the foreign ownership issue is wider than just its incidence in the producing sector of the petroleum industry and if we were to explicitly acknowledge it we would have to calculate the extent to which foreign owners in the energy consumption sector gain via blended oil pricing.

VI. PRICING OF NATURAL GAS

A surprising inconsistency

In the case of natural gas, the price mechanism emerges in the NEP as a fundamental motivating force.

> "Pricing policy for natural gas must meet two needs: provision of adequate incentive to production, and strong encouragement for consumers to use natural gas in preference to oil. . . Thus the challenge is to find means whereby the producers' desire to expand markets can be addressed through determined efforts to increase dramatically the use of natural gas in Canada at the expense of oil. This requires attractive price incentives to the consumer. . . Gas prices to the consumer will, however, rise less quickly than oil prices in order to encourage a shift away from oil to natural gas."[20]

In other words, while pricing does not seem to be particularly favoured as a means of stimulating oil conservation — at least over the near term — it is reinstated as a force to impel the substitution of gas for oil. In this sense, the NEP is right to say:

> "Linking Canadian natural gas prices to world oil prices is also unwise, because Canadian endowments of oil and gas resources differ. . . Linking Canadian prices to world prices could keep the price of gas to the consumer rising at the same rate as the price of oil. This would inhibit the massive-scale substitution away from oil that must take place if Canada is to achieve energy security.[21]

This implies the previous policy of linking oil and gas prices via the 85 per cent rule at Toronto is an anachronism — which it is.

The NEP seeks to impose a lower natural gas price *vis à vis* the price of oil by regulatory fiat. Relatively lower natural gas pricing is consistent with the direction market pressures would seem to dictate, given the combination of quite abundant supplies of natural gas and restrictions on its export. The change in relative price relationships is

TABLE V
AN ESTIMATE OF OIL SUPPLY EFFICIENCY LOSSES BLENDED OIL PRICING REGIME, 1984
(all $ figures are $ Canadian)

1.[1]	1984 oil production	544 million bbls/year
2.[2]	Representative domestic oil net back price Edmonton	$30.54 per bbl.
3.[3]	Representative world oil net back price, Edmonton	$63.49 per bbl.
4.	Implicit per barrel subsidy = (3 – 2)	$32.95 per bbl.
5.	Value of production (1 × 2)	$16,613 million/year
6.[4]	Estimated additional production at world prices	134 million bbls/year
7.	Estimated production at world price (1 + 6)	678 million bbls/year
8.	Implicit benefits on additional production (6 × 3)	$8,508 million/year
9.[5]	Implicit costs of additional production	$6,300 million/year
	of which 9a cost at domestic price (2 × 6)	$4,092 million/year
	9b incremental cost ½ (4 × 6)	$2,208 million/year
10.	Efficiency cost of foregoing additional production (8 – 9)	$2,208 million/year

Notes:
1. Various forecasts.
2. Comprises weighted average Alberta wellhead price plus gathering costs to Edmonton.
3. Toronto world oil price less transportation costs from Edmonton.
4. Assumes price elasticity of 0.3
5. Assumes linear supply curve over this period.

essential to shift demand from a commodity in short supply (oil) to one with which we are richly endowed. How closely the regulated price would approximate a more freely determined market price is an open question. The freeing of domestic gas producer prices would provide this answer without government intervention, as the prices would gravitate toward the levels dictated by the underlying oil and gas supply-demand realities. However, reliance on a competitive market solution is out of kilter with the essentially interventionist character of the NEP. Instead, selective pricing measures are advocated. Transportation of gas to new Eastern markets is to be subsidized and other kinds of subsidies are proposed.[22]

In short, natural gas marketing is to be quasi-monopolistic in character. Gas prices in Eastern markets will not reflect differential transportation costs. Lower prices are to be charged in new markets to entice new customers while existing customers will be charged a higher price. In short, a policy of price discrimination is endorsed.

VII. CONCLUDING REMARKS

In the NEP, the main function of the pricing mechanism to act as an arbiter of economic efficiency in resource allocation has been emasculated. Instead, pricing tends to be seen more as a vehicle for revenue sharing between governments.[23] Its original function is lost in a welter of special arrangements, incentives and programs, especially in the case of oil.

The signals emanating from the world oil market are to be ignored or suppressed by the NEP. Average or blended pricing is to be employed in domestic markets, which will only transmit to consumers in a muted way the economic cost of consumption decisions, as long as imports represent the marginal source of supply. Imports will be higher than at world prices; consequently, costs will be imposed on the economy. However, the blended oil pricing scheme will be an improvement over the present arrangements, whereby oil consumers are totally shielded from the substantial differences between the cost of domestic supplies and the cost of oil imports. The deadweight loss for the economy associated with the NEP pricing arrangements amounts to $1.2 billion.

In terms of stimulating supply, heavy reliance is to be placed on discriminatory pricing, with government administrators judging what price is needed to entice new supplies. New supplies of conventional oil other than from tertiary recovery mechanisms will not qualify for favourable treatment. Tertiary recovery, oil sands and possibly frontier oil will be rewarded. In other words, some new supplies are to be more equal than others. This sort of price discrimination will engender economic losses to the economy by discouraging development of certain types of supply. Some resources will be lost, other developments may be deferred, perhaps indefinitely. The timing of resource additions may be less than optimal. Initial selective pricing may well lead to a greater and more cumbersome degree of selectivity. The costs of administration of this kind of scheme and blended oil pricing are by no means trivial. The deadweight losses are estimated to be $2.2 billion.

Reliance on relative prices to encourage substitution of natural gas for oil is endorsed by the NEP, and given constraints on exports of gas this is a sensible recognition of the more prolific current endowment of gas in Canada. However, in the next few years producer prices for domestic gas, after adjustment for inflation, will remain at much the same level as they are now. In other words, additional gas supply is to be discouraged, presumably on the grounds that present supplies are adequate or even excessive. Although we can only speculate as to the actual outcome it seems unlikely this sort of answer would emerge from freeing up domestic gas prices in conjunction with an alignment of oil prices to world levels. The NEP seeks to impose this regime by regulation, without the knowledge that would arise from relying on the market mechanism.

Of the various price provisions in the NEP, the desire to dissociate domestic prices from world prices is the one most likely to induce costs on the economy not offset by corresponding benefits. Ignoring the world oil market will tend to prevent Canada from pursuing vigorous development of potential supplies of all forms of energy. In other words, the opportunities created for Canada by current and future levels of international oil prices may well be squandered. And our vulnerability to shocks emanating from the world oil market is increased.

FOOTNOTES

1 See Department of Energy, Mines and Resources, "An Energy Strategy for Canada: Policies for Self Reliance", Ottawa, 1976, p. 147.

2 In 1976, the delivered price of world oil at Montreal was $13 per barrel ($ Canadian) and the delivered price of domestic oil was $9.35 per barrel; in November 1980 the corresponding numbers were $39 and $19.70.

3 Department of Energy, Mines and Resources, "National Energy Program", Ottawa November 1980 (hereafter abbreviated as NEP).

4 Tertiary recovery means additional crude oil recovery from petroleum reservoirs through the application of third generation enhanced recovery methods: the newer, less technically proven techniques.

5 NEP, p. 29.

6 NEP, p. 51.

7 NEP, p. 27.

8 For example, see NEP, pp. 4, 5, 23.

9 H. Hotelling, "Economics of Exhaustible Resources", *Journal of Political Economy*, 1931.

10 For example, see B.A. Kalymon, "Economic incentives in OPEC oil pricing policy", *Journal of Development Economics*, Vol. 2, No. 4, 1975, pp. 337-361; J. Cremer and M.L. Weitzman, "OPEC and the monopoly price of world oil", *European Economic Review*, Vol. 8, 1976, pp. 155-164; E. Hnyilicza and R.S. Pindyck, "Pricing policies for a two-part exhaustible resource cartel", *European Economic Review*, Vol. 8, 1976, pp. 139-154; W.J. Mead, "An Economic Analysis of Crude Oil Price Behaviour in the 70's", *Journal of Energy and Development, Spring 1979*; and U.S. Department of Energy, "A Sensitivity Analysis of World Oil Prices", September 1979.

11 NEP, p. 7.

12 See J.G. Stabback's essay in this volume.

13 See other essays in this volume.

14 In the short run, responses are constrained by existing stocks of equipment, automobiles, boilers and the like, but in the longer run these are malleable.

15 An adjustment has been made to reflect refining and distribution margins and petroleum product taxes in calculating this consumption variation. The increase in refinery gate blended prices of oil to reach world levels would be over 55 per cent. After including 1984 margins and taxes of $11.00 per barrel, the corresponding rise in the price of petroleum products would be 43 per cent.

16 NEP, p. 24.

17 NEP, p. 24.

18 This may well be an underestimate in the sense that it excludes supply responses in other energy sources which would be stimulated by higher prices for them as a function of higher oil prices. This applies primarily to natural gas and coal, and to a lesser extent, electricity.

19 See G.C. Watkins, "Canadian Oil Pricing: An Immaculate Deception?", *University of Calgary Conference Proceedings*, "Energy: Coping in the 1980's", forthcoming. In turn, those calculations are based on B. Scarfe and B. Wilkinson, "The Recycling Problem", *Energy Policies for the 1980s: An Economic Analysis*, Ontario Economic Council, Vol. 1, 1980.

20 NEP, p. 31.

21 NEP, p. 24.

22 NEP, pp. 57-59.

23 At one stage, the NEP (p. 21) treats the basic point as "what is the appropriate distribution of oil and gas revenues among governments".

24 In other words, the impacts are dynamic rather than static.

Chapter 4

The National Energy Program and Fiscal Federalism: Some Observations

THOMAS J. COURCHENE
Department of Economics
University of Western Ontario
London

THE AUTHOR

THOMAS J. COURCHENE is Professor of Economics at the University of Western Ontario. Born in Saskatchewan in 1940, he was educated at the University of Saskatchewan and received his Ph.D. from Princeton University in 1967. He has also been Professor in Residence at the Graduate Institute of International Studies in Geneva, and has done postgraduate study at the University of Chicago. Professor Courchene has been a member of the editorial boards of the *Journal of Money, Credit and Banking* and the *Canadian Journal of Economics*. He is a member of the Editorial Advisory Board of the Fraser Institute, and is a Fellow of the C.D. Howe Research Institute.

Professor Courchene is author of many books, articles, and reviews, including: "Energy and Equalization," in *Energy Policies for 1980s and Economic Analyses*, Ontario Economic Council, 1979; "Towards a Protected Society: Politicization of Economic Life," (The Innis Memorial Lecture), *Canadian Journal of Economics*, 1980; "Post-Controls and the Public Sector" in *Which Way Ahead?* published by the Fraser Institute; and "Avenues of Adjustment: The Transfer System and Regional Disparities," *Canadian Confederation at the Crossroads*, published by the Fraser Institute.

He has also written several studies for the C.D. Howe Research Institute, including: *Money, Inflation and the Bank of Canada: An Analysis of Canadian Monetary Policy from 1970 to Early 1975* (1976), *Monetarism and Controls: The Inflation Fighters* (1976), *The Strategy of Gradualism: An Analysis of Bank of Canada Policy from Mid-1975 to Mid-1977* (1977), and *Refinancing the Canadian Federation: The 1977 Fiscal Arrangement* (October 1979).

The National Energy Program and Fiscal Federalism: Some Observations

THOMAS J. COURCHENE

Department of Economics
University of Western Ontario
London

I. INTRODUCTION

The purpose of this paper is to attempt to evaluate some of the federal-provincial fiscal implications of the 1980 budget or, more precisely, of the 1980 National Energy Program (NEP). The initial step in this evaluation is an analysis of the impact of the energy crisis on the various parts of the Canadian federation. This will provide the necessary backdrop to isolate those issues in the federal-provincial arena that were generating concern, *pre-budget*. The remainder of the paper will focus on selected measures of the NEP and how they are likely to impinge on the selected range of federal-provincial issues. A short conclusion, including my preferences as to what the NEP should have included, completes the analysis.

At the outset, it is important to recognize that this will be a very broad-ranging analysis. My expertise is that of an economic analyst. However, almost of necessity the range of issues broached by the NEP embroils one into the intricacies of the related fields of federalism and constitutional law. I will not shy away from expressing some opinions in these areas, but the reader should be aware that in doing so I am exceeding the bounds of my own discipline. Finally, even when it comes to the economic issues, the bulk of the analysis often boils down to arguments relating to income distribution or "rent sharing", to use the appropriate jargon. This being the case, the role of the economist is circumscribed since income distribution questions are beyond the confines of traditional economic analysis. Put somewhat differently, major elements of what follows are best interpreted as the views of an informed layman — they cannot be derived from basic economic principles.

II. PETRO-DOLLARS AND THE PROVINCES: A BACKGROUND TO THE ANALYSIS

A. THE EFFECT OF RISING ENERGY PRICES[1]

From an economic standpoint, the rising price of energy is best viewed as an increase in the terms of trade (the ratio of export prices to import prices) of the energy-producing provinces and a fall in the terms of trade of the non-energy-producing provinces. For simplicity, I shall refer to these groups of provinces as the West and East, respectively. The immediate impact of the terms-of-trade change will be a transfer of real income from the East to the West. This is so because a given volume of energy exports from the West will now purchase a larger volume of imports from the East. If production remains unchanged, residents of the East must reduce their real consumption or dip into previous savings, while for residents in the West both consumption and wealth will rise. Production is not likely to remain unchanged, however. Petroleum is an important input into many production processes and thus the price of manufactures will rise, which will serve to reduce the real incomes of residents in both the East and West. This may have further effects in the East where manufactures are exported abroad, depending on the differential impact of energy on domestic and foreign costs. On this score the real transfer from East to West is mitigated to the extent that Canada's domestic price is held below world levels. A low domestic price implies that a substantial portion of the resource rents from the energy sector are accruing to consumers (either directly in the form of lower heating and transportation costs or indirectly in the form of lower prices for products which embody energy in their production) rather than to the resource producers or to governments.

Production will be further influenced if the terms-of-trade shift results in the migration of factors of production. With higher prices for petroleum, and for energy generally, rates of return in this sector will rise and this will result in an increased flow of capital to the energy sector which, in the short run at least, essentially implies a flow to the West. Because of the increased wealth of the West and partly because migration will lead to an increased population base for the West, there will also be an increased flow of non-energy capital to the West.

Transportation costs will rise as energy prices climb and the impact of this is similar to that of a tariff — it will encourage industry to locate in or near the West in order to avoid this tariff, i.e., the high transport costs. It is in this sense that I can see a larger supply and distribution role for Manitoba over the longer run as a provider of labour-intensive manufactures to the West at the expense of central Canada.

B. EFFECTING THE WEALTH TRANSFER

Over the longer term this transfer of purchasing power will be made in "real" terms — easterners will pay for their oil imports through an increase in exports, either to the West or the rest of the world. Essentially, therefore, net exports of the East (i.e., production in the East minus domestic absorption in the East) must rise in order to generate the increased real outflow associated with oil imports. Failure to make the transfer in "real terms" implies that the East is continually borrowing from or steadily selling its assets to the West — an untenable position over the longer haul.

In the short run, however, the transfer of purchasing power will be effected principally in terms of *financial* flows. The fact that the East and the West are part of the same currency union greatly facilitates the financial transfers — residents of the East or their governments will simply draw down savings or increase their borrowings either from the West or the rest of the world in order to cover the balance of payments deficit with the West. Indeed, this common currency aspect of the financial adjustment is what differentiates the short-term adjustment process in Canada from that which characterized the transfer arising from the "German Reparations" issue. In the latter case, the recipient countries were, in general, not willing to hold the German currency so that Germany was forced to make the adjustment in "real" terms, even in the shorter term.

Yet the fact that the short-run adjustment is facilitated by the existence of a currency union may well exacerbate the longer-term adjustment. Easterners may not realize the true magnitude of the required *real* adjustment and their efforts to maintain consumption levels either by dipping into savings or, more likely, by having their governments run larger deficits over a prolonged period, may well result in reductions in their wealth to lower levels than would have been the case had the real adjustment been effected more quickly.

Therefore, with exchange rate adjustment between the East and the West ruled out, the burden of the transfer must take place through other channels. Wages will rise (and have risen) in the West relative to the East. A fall in relative wages in the East will a) enhance exports to and capital investment from the West b) increase output in the East and/or encourage labour to move westward. All of these will help effect the real transfer. Naturally, there will be a tendency for Easterners to attempt to have their wages move upward in tandem with those in the West. To the extent that this occurs it is difficult to escape the reality that the unemployment rate in the East is going to rise substantially. This creates its own problems but as well it makes the ultimate adjustment all the more severe. A fall in output arising from increased unemployment means that the wealth of the East is going to have to be drawn down *even further* in order to free the exports to effect the transfer in real terms.

This then is a brief overview of the impact of rising energy prices on the geographical allocation or reallocation of economic power within the Canadian federation. It is, of course, highly abstract in the sense that I have omitted many important factors. For example, I did not refer to the direct impact on Ontario of the structural crisis in the auto industry in the wake of mushrooming world energy prices. Nor did I refer to the fact that the combination of supply constraints and capitalization of the energy wealth have led to tremendous increases in the value of real estate in the West, in effect generating a substantial entry price for migrants. Moreover, little or no mention was made of the fact that a strong and growing energy sector implies that the East will be a major supplier of intermediate products to this sector. Nonetheless, I believe that the above analysis captures the essence of the energy scenario as it relates to the distribution of economic activity in the federation. In a word, the centre of economic activity is moving rapidly westward. Naturally, the degree of westward shift has been moderated because Canada has chosen to hold the domestic price of energy well below the world price.

With this as backdrop, I now want to focus on some of the important issues in the area of federal-provincial fiscal relations that the energy crisis has either generated or exacerbated. In a later section I explore the implications of the NEP on these same issues.

III. PROBLEM AREAS IN FISCAL FEDERALISM

A. RENT SHARING AND THE PRICE OF ENERGY

First and foremost, there is the rent-sharing issue. Under the pre-existing arrangements the federal share of energy rents approximated 10 per cent, with the remaining 90 per cent split roughly evenly between the industry and the producing provinces.† This oft-quoted allocation is not carved in stone. Rather it represents the experience over the last few years. For example, in order for the industry to keep its share as high as 45 per cent, it would have to invest in exploration and development a large percentage of any gross revenue increase. Failure to do so would imply substantially higher corporate taxes. Thus, were the price of energy to rise substantially under the old arrangements it is likely that Ottawa's share of the incremental energy resources would be much larger than 10 per cent, simply because of the difficulty for the industry to generate sufficient exploration and development activity.

Nonetheless, it was clear that Ottawa's share of energy resources was small, not only in relation to the provinces' share but also in relation to Ottawa's expenditures relating to energy. Elsewhere, I have detailed some of the federal revenues and expenditures associated with non-renewable energy resources.[2] Suffice it to say that the combined federal expenditures on energy-related equalization payments and the oil import compensation program exceeded by a large margin the amount of revenue Ottawa derived from the energy sector.[3]

I think it should have been clear to everyone, Alberta included, that Ottawa was going to garner a larger share of the energy revenues. The only unresolved questions were how and how much.

Ottawa's arguments for a larger share

There are no doubt many possible arguments for a greater federal share of the energy pie. I want to touch on three of them. The first

†Editor's Note: While this is the conventional view of shares, the reader should consult the paper by Professor Norrie in this volume for an alternative view which includes in the federal share the implicit subsidy provided to consumers in the form of lower prices.

relates to the proposition that Ottawa "deserves" more. Specifically, the federal government has provided the energy sector with literally billions of dollars in terms of corporate tax writeoffs and/or tax deferrals for exploration, drilling, etc. Yet as soon as oil or gas is discovered the provinces tend to assume that the revenues belong to them, not to Ottawa. A second variant of this argument is that Ottawa's generous exploration provisions have been capitalized in the values of the bids for Crown leases, which have generated close to a billion dollars for the producing provinces in some years. This amounts to a straightforward transfer from the federal to the provincial treasuries. The third rationale is essentially that the provincial governments simply could not expect to pocket all the energy rents. Ottawa has to shoulder the major responsibility for activities in the areas of energy conservation, energy alternatives, the economic fallout in the non-energy region of the country, etc. and it could not tolerate the existing allocation of revenues between itself and the provinces.

Table I presents some estimates of the amount of money at stake. The data in the table relate to the impact of a $1 per barrel increase in the price of domestic energy (the price of natural gas is assumed to increase by 15¢ per Mcf). From row 1, the cost to consuming Canadians (consumption assumed to remain constant) is $890 million. Royalties accruing to the producing provinces would total $420 million with $362 million of this accruing to Alberta (row 2). Underlying these figures is the assumption that the aggregate energy sector revenues will amount to $1 billion from this dollar-per-barrel increase, so that federal revenues would be in the neighbourhood of $100 million. This $100 million is barely enough to cover Ottawa's increased equalization payments and indeed would *not* cover incremental equalization burden if Ontario were deemed to be eligible to receive equalization. More on the equalization implications later.

When one considers that, at the time this table was constructed, Canadian oil prices were roughly $20 below world level, the financial implications for the internal transfer of going to world prices with existing rent-sharing arrangements were enormous. (It would probably be wrong to multiply the figures in the table by 20 because consumption would not remain unchanged, but the magnitudes would be staggering in any event.) There are, however, indirect financial implications for Ottawa of a rising domestic energy price. As the world price-domestic price gap is closed, Ottawa saves revenues because it

TABLE I

A 'BALANCE SHEET' FOR A $1 PER BARREL RISE IN THE PRICE OF DOMESTIC ENERGY

Rising energy prices and macro adjustment[a]

	Nfld.	PEI	NS	NB	Que.	Ont.	Man.	Sask.	Alta.	BC	Total
1. Cost to provinces ($ millions)[b]	18.1	3.9	35.9	30.8	199.2	323.2	30.0	40.5	123.1	86.0	890.7
2. Royalties for producing provinces ($ millions)[c]						.9	1.5	28.0	361.8	28.6	420.8
3. Resulting equalization payment increase ($ millions)[d]	5.1	1.0	7.6	6.3	56.2	0[g]	8.3	-6.4	0	0	78.1
4. Funding allocation for equalization ($ millions)[e]	1.1	0.2	1.9	1.5	18.4	30.2	2.8	2.6	9.4	10.0	78.1
5. 'Net balance' ($ millions)[d]	-14.2	-3.1	-30.2	-26.0	-161.4	-352.3	-23.0	-21.5	+229.3	-67.4	
6. Source of federal revenue (%)[f]	1.38	0.28	2.40	1.90	23.60	38.87	3.60	3.37	12.01	12.79	100%

[a] Adapted from Courchene and Melvin, *op. cit.*, p. 195.

[b] These are based on 1978 consumption levels and are calculated as the sum of the costs of crude oil and its equivalent, natural gas, and LPG's. The crude oil consumption levels by province are taken from the December 1978 issue of *Refined Petroleum Products* (Statistics Canada, 45-004) Table 3 (utilizing 'domestic disappearance'). Natural gas consumption by province is taken from the December 1978 issue of *Crude Petroleum and Natural Gas Production* (Statistics Canada: 26-006), Table 5, lines 18 through 24. Data for LPG consumption by province (net of that reported from the crude oil and equivalent sources) was estimated from NEB data. The price of natural gas was assumed to increase by 85 per cent of the heat equivalent increase in oil. Specifically $1 per barrel increase in oil was assumed and a 14.65 cent increase (per Mcf) in natural gas.

[c] Assumes roughly $1 billion in revenues to the oil and gas industry. Royalties are assumed to average 42 per cent, yielding the $420.8 million total. Revenues from corporate income taxes are excluded for this calculation. Gas equivalent price increase assumed to be 15 cents Mcf.

[d] Assumes Ontario will not receive equalization payments. The net balance equals 2 + 3 - 1 - 4.

[e] Allocated according to the shares in 6.

[f] These shares were calculated as follows: Ottawa's tax revenues come principally from three sources: personal income taxes, corporate income taxes and indirect taxes. We then made the simplifying assumption that all of Ottawa's revenues come from these three sources. Next we allocated provincial shares of these taxes according to the tax base shares (derived from the equalization tables) for personal income taxes, business income taxes and general sales taxes respectively. The provincial shares in row 6 are the result of applying weights (summing to unity and based on the share of federal revenue) and summing the three provincial revenue categories.

[g] Ontario is a have-not province, but thus far no equalization funds have been paid to it. If payments were allowed, the figure for Ontario would be $75.4 million.

will be spending less in terms of the oil import subsidy program, which is currently running about $3 billion.

The Alberta position

The position of the West, and in particular of Alberta, on rent sharing is not without merit either. There are at least two ways to portray this position. The first one focuses on the very same data that were reviewed in the previous section. For each dollar the Canadian price is below world prices, Alberta is "foregoing" nearly $400 million in revenues per year. Under this view, Alberta has contributed billions of dollars over the past few years to the rest of Canada. This argument is airtight, provided a) one accepts the world price as the appropriate reference price (which I do) and b) one accepts the existing revenue-sharing arrangements as appropriate. The latter is a big proviso, however.

The second approach is more general. It goes roughly as follows. If Alberta is allowed to set the price for energy, then it will supply all the energy that Ottawa demands. If Ottawa sets the price, then Alberta wants to be able to set the quantity it will supply at this price. What Alberta is not willing to do is have Ottawa set *both* the energy price and the quantity it must supply at this price. I accept this approach as valid. In effect, it is nothing more than a statement of the right of Alberta as owner of the resource to set a reservation price. *But it really says nothing at all about rent sharing.* For example, I own the services of my labour and, therefore, I have the right to withhold them if I deem that the wage rate offered is not appropriate. But that does not mean that Ottawa and the provinces do not have the right to levy taxes on the labour income I receive.

One could carry on *ad infinitum* on rent sharing, focusing on the constitutional rights of both parties, the precedents established by existing arrangements, etc. But when all is said and done, revenue-sharing is an income distribution issue and as such it will be resolved in the political arena (or perhaps in the courts). My own view is that even Alberta recognized that the option of moving close to world price levels with the pre-existing rent-sharing arrangement was simply not in the cards — the federal government was going to get a larger share.

B. EQUALIZATION

Rising energy revenues since 1973 have forced major changes in Canada's system of equalization payments, so much so that they made the program increasingly arbitrary. These alterations have been detailed elsewhere.[4] The problem was rather straightforward. Despite the fact that the *philosophy* of equalization was cast in terms of transferring funds to provinces so that they could provide some average level of public services without resorting to unduly high levels of taxation, the *implementation* of the system focused on ensuring that all provinces had access to the national-average level of provincial revenues. With energy revenues soaring in Alberta, Ottawa found itself with an increasingly large equalization expenditure.[5] Despite the many specific provisions designed to minimize the influence of energy revenues on the equalization system, Ontario became a have-not province in fiscal year 1976-77 and has maintained this status ever since. No money has actually been paid to Ontario because of provisions agreed upon in 1977 (but which have never received Royal assent). The accumulated amount now owed to Ontario for equalization is fast approaching $1 billion and, after the next election, Ontario is likely to demand payment.

There is a further aspect of the equalization program that presents particular problems for Ontario. This is evident from Table I. As noted above, the impact on Ontario residents of a $1 per barrel energy price hike is in the neighbourhood of $325 million. Equalization payments rise by $78.1 million (row 3). Ontario's residents contribute about 40 per cent of the total financing of the program (row 6), so that the additional cost to Ontario is $30 million dollars (row 4). The net result is that even though Ontario falls into the category of a have-not province, the manner in which the present equalization program works means that Ontario's overall burden relating to energy price increases is *exacerbated* by the operations of the equalization program. Professors Flatters and Purvis of Queen's University have argued that the distortions to factor mobility that the combination of the current energy rent-sharing arrangements and the operation of the equalization program would provide are such that it would be *allocatively inefficient* to go to world price levels without adjusting one or both of these programs.[6]†

†Editor's Note: The Flatters-Purvis paper is subjected to critical review in Professor Norrie's paper in this volume.

The time has come to rethink some aspects of the equalization program. The program comes up for review in the spring of 1982 and now that the parameters of the NEP are known, it should be possible to make some progress in this direction. However, while I have raised this as a current issue and have no doubt that the NEP will influence its redesign, I alert the reader ahead of time that I will have little light to shed on this issue in later parts of the paper.

C. SECURING AN INTERNAL COMMON MARKET

The energy crisis heightened several aspects of what has come to be known as the Canadian common market issue, i.e., the degree to which goods, services, capital and labour can move freely across provincial boundaries. This issue dominated much of this past summer's round of Constitutional talks. Obviously, the concern for an internal common market is much broader than the manner in which the energy problem relates to it, but it is the energy-related aspects that are of interest for present purposes. Perhaps the most direct link between energy and the common market issue is Newfoundland's attempt to ensure that Newfoundland residents have first crack at off-shore drilling jobs. The more subtle aspects are probably more important and to these I now turn.

In the very heated debate that took place on this issue over the summer, it became clear that often there were ulterior (i.e., self-interest) motives that became hard to disentangle from the economic or constitutional aspects of the problem. Ontario provides a good example. Very early in the talks, Ontario sided with Ottawa in the pursuit of an internal common market, particularly as it related to the elimination of government purchasing preferences. Given the immense investment projects that are (or *were*, pre-budget) about to commence in Alberta, Ontario is also anxious to compete on an equal footing with domestic (Western) industry for these contracts. It even went as far at one stage to admit its previous "error" in awarding a large contract to a Northern Ontario concern rather than to Bombardier (of Quebec) which had the lowest bid. However, there was a "rider" implicitly attached to its position, namely that Ottawa would at the same time push for a "buy Canadian" preference. This would then put Ontario industry in an enviable position *vis-à-vis* other Canadian provinces when it came to supplying and servicing the Alberta boom. Whatever Ontario's true motives for pushing the common market viewpoint, it nonetheless came to be viewed by many participants as a self-interest stance and, in principle, not very different from the points of view that are taken by the various participants in the NEP itself.

Another example is Quebec's personal income tax deductions for residents who purchase new issues of Quebec-based companies. This may not relate directly to the westward movement of capital, but it does represent a significant fragmentation in the national market for capital and if it were to be copied by other provinces would pose a very serious impediment. Along the same lines, Alberta is currently in the process of patriating its corporate income tax system, thereby joining the ranks of Ontario and Quebec who also collect their own corporate taxes. The fear, perhaps totally unfounded, is that Alberta may use the tax as a vehicle for attracting industry to the province not so much by lowering tax rates as by abandoning its adherence to the allocation formula that distributes corporate profits of interprovincial enterprises across the various provinces. Thus far, all provinces adhere to a common allocation formula and the elimination of such a formula would amount to a substantial erosion of the internal economic union. I shall argue later in the paper that the NEP provides further incentives in this direction.

D. HERITAGE FUNDS AND PUBLIC ENTERPRISE

Another area that concerns me a great deal (although thus far not many Canadians have shared the concern) is the substantial incentive that exists for the "provincialization" of profit making institutions. Section 125 of the *BNA Act* appears to prohibit one level of government from taxing the other so that there exists a tremendous advantage for provinces to establish their own enterprises, thereby avoiding federal tax. An example or two will illustrate the point I want to make. The Heritage Fund pays no federal tax on the near-billion-dollar interest revenue from its assets. How long will it be before a major financial institution cries "foul" because the Heritage Fund outbids it for a loan placement? More intriguing still, suppose the Heritage Fund were to buy Massey-Ferguson and turn it into a profit-making institution. Neither Ottawa nor Ontario would then have any right to tax the profits of Massey-Ferguson. This general issue is eventually going to have to be resolved and I shall argue below that the NEP will hasten the day of reckoning.

E. THE DIVISION OF POWERS: THE POLITICAL DIMENSION

These, then, are some of the issues that in my opinion were simmering, pre-budget, in the federal-provincial fiscal arena. Others may obviously have selected a quite different list. Most of the remainder of the paper will focus on the manner in which the NEP is likely to impinge on these concerns. Prior to embarking on this exercise, however, it is critical to recognize that underlying all of these concerns and the manner in which they interact with the NEP is the major political issue of the division of power between the federal government and the provinces. Many of the provinces tend to view the budget and the NEP as simply the second round of the federal Constitutional package. As such, it becomes extremely difficult to disentangle the political from the economic issues, assuming that this would be possible in the first place. In order to put the political overtones of the NEP in some sort of perspective, I want to quote at length from a post-budget speech delivered by Toronto lawyer, W.A. Macdonald:

> "The federal budget last night was a Budget with a capital P—Politics and Power. The voice was that of the Minister of Finance. But, one must conclude, the words were those of the Energy Minister and of the Prime Minister.
>
> . . . The key to understanding the risks in the present situation is less the substance of the constitutional, energy and budget proposals, important as these are, than the choice by the federal government of the unilateral way to their achievement. The justifiability of this choice and the ultimate consequence of having made it may well override the debate on the merits or demerits of these proposals in the period ahead.
>
> . . . By choosing the unilateral way, the federal government strips the concerned provinces of their bargaining leverage at the table. What it is saying is that it can get what it wants without them. The risk is that this provokes the unavoidable question of whether one wants to continue at a table where one's chips don't count in the game . . .
>
> In the case of the Constitution, this raises the question of whether the federal government can in fact get its way without throwing away the long-standing rules of the Constitutional game in Canada — and whether "if" it can throw away the rules for its own purposes, others may not feel that they can do the same for theirs."[7]

I support fully these perceptive remarks by W.A. Macdonald. The impact of the energy policy goes well beyond the individual features (some of which are listed below) of the program. The concept of federalism as a system of "self-rule, shared-rule" was shattered in the budget. It may well be the case that there was no possibility that Ottawa and the energy provinces could come to any common understanding. It is also the case that many Canadians, probably even many Albertans, can sympathize with the federal government's general goals such as acquiring a larger share of energy rents. But the budget appears to many of those same people (myself included) as saying that the *ends justify the means*. This is diametrically opposed to the tradition of Canadian federalism. At the limit, the budget represents an abrupt movement away from federalism and towards the notion of a unitary state.

My purpose in raising these issues is not to shed insight on the future evolution of Canadian federalism. I am not an expert in this area. However, it is very clear that the unilateral approach to energy policy is going to have severe repercussions on the range of problem areas in fiscal federalism that I outlined earlier. Moreover, in the heated debate in which the country is now embroiled it is probably the case that the form as much as the substance of the NEP is at issue.

IV. SALIENT FEATURES OF THE NATIONAL ENERGY PROGRAM FOR FISCAL FEDERALISM

There is no question that the NEP is the most important piece of legislation in the economic and political sphere that Canada has seen in a good long while. The comprehensive system of levies and taxes on the one hand and energy-related expenditures on the other will not only have a major impact on the energy sector but as well they hold significant implications for the division of power between Ottawa and the provinces and for the role of public sector involvement in economic activity. My purpose here is not to review the program in its entirety. Rather, it is to focus on these aspects that will likely have lasting repercussions on federal-provincial relations. Obviously, however, this is a difficult and perhaps impossible task since the reactions of the producing provinces and Canadians generally are influenced by the overall program and not simply by these measures that might be viewed as infringing specifically upon the fiscal interactions between the two levels of government.

A. PRICING

Beginning in 1981 and through to 1983 the wellhead price will increase by only $2 per barrel per year. From 1983 to 1985 the price will rise by $4.50 per year and from 1986 to 1989 by $7 per year. Even larger increases are forecast beginning in 1990 if the domestic price remains significantly below the world price. The price at the "pump", however, will also increase by $4.50 per year until 1983 because Ottawa will apply a Petroleum Compensation Charge of $2.50 per year that will be in addition to the $2 per barrel wellhead increase. This is the "blended price" concept whereby Canadians will be taxed at the pump in order to cover the costs of the higher-priced imported oil. By 1990 the wellhead price will be $66.75 compared to a value, pre-budget, of $16.75 — a four-fold increase. To this must be added the roughly $8 per barrel arising from the Petroleum Compensation Charge as well as any future per barrel taxes that would be used to finance any nationalization of existing foreign-owned companies.

This gradual approach to higher energy prices will obviously not sit well with those who argue for a "cold-turkey" approach in going to world prices. However, it should be noted that it is a marked improvement on the status quo and it finally provides a longer-term planning horizon for Canadian consumers and industries alike. My own view is that world oil prices are not likely to rise in real terms over the next decade. I base this on my belief that decontrol in the U.S. will finally pay dividends in terms of U.S. domestic supply and, therefore, on the world energy price.

From Alberta's standpoint (and the producing provinces generally), the concerns over pricing are probably two-fold. First of all, the wellhead increase is very minimal over the next 3 years. Secondly, and more important for the federation, the federal government has moved *unilaterally* to establish energy prices, the vehicle for this intrusion being the *Petroleum Administrative Act*. In his post-budget speech, Premier Lougheed acknowledged that he had probably lost the pricing battle. However, the problem with unilaterally set prices is that they can also be changed unilaterally.

Of and by itself, the pricing decision could probably have been accepted by the West provided the rest of the arrangements remained intact. But they did not.

B. RENT-SHARING

There was no way that rent-sharing would not be a critical issue in any energy package. After all, rent-sharing between Ottawa and the provinces is a zero-sum game — what Ottawa gains, the producing provinces lose, and vice-versa. Under the old arrangements the average revenue allocations were 45:45:10 for the industry, the provincial governments and the federal government, respectively. Over the period 1980-1983, the new arrangements imply an allocation of 33:43:24 for the industry, the provinces and Ottawa.[8] (NEP, p. 108.) Moreover, the above figures are averages over 1980-1983. For 1983 itself, the allocation is even more in Ottawa's favour since some of the taxes (particularly on gas) rise over time, i.e., 32:40:28. This represents a massive rent transfer which, combined with the niggardly wellhead increase over the next three years has left the producing provinces, particularly Alberta, livid. In addition, the above figures do *not* take account of the substantial federal revenues that will be generated by the excise tax levied under the umbrella of the Petroleum Compensation Charge, referred to earlier. This money does not in the first instance flow to the energy sector, which is probably why it is not included in the calculations. At any rate, by 1983 Ottawa will likely be garnering as much from energy as will the provinces. It is useful to focus on two of the new sources of Ottawa's funds.

The first is the tax on natural gas and gas liquids. By 1983 the value of this tax will be the equivalent of $5 per barrel (i.e., 75¢ per Mcf). This tax would be less irksome to the provinces were it not for the fact that for 1981, for example, Ottawa is not allowing any wellhead increase for the price of natural gas. Indeed, to the end of 1983, wellhead prices will increase by only 60¢ per Mcf.

My own view on the general strategy relating to the pricing of natural gas is that it is absurd to tie it to the heat equivalent price for oil, as Canada has done in the past. After all gas and oil are not perfect substitutes and we have lots of gas and a shortage of oil. We do not price liver on the basis of the protein equivalent of steak! Ideally, the price of gas should be allowed to find its own value in the domestic market and this should imply a significantly lower price than prevails for oil. In effect, the budget moves in this direction in the sense that in 1980 the price of gas equalled 80 per cent of the Btu price of oil and by 1983 this will fall to 67 per cent (NEP, p. 32). From the producing provinces' (Alberta and British Columbia) point of view, however, this is no doubt viewed as a direct transfer from them to the federal coffers.

The second major tax initiative was the 8 per cent levy on the net operating revenues related to the production of oil and gas, including income from oil and gas royalty interests. Apart from being a major new intrusion into the energy sector, there are two aspects of this tax that are particularly relevant for present purposes. First of all, this 8 per cent is an *initial* levy (NEP, p. 38), which has been established for the period over which gas and oil will increase by \$1 per barrel every 6 months — that is until 1983. After that, the wellhead price of oil will increase by \$4.50 per year, and later by \$7 per year. The clear implication left in the NEP is that this levy will *increase* in line with the larger wellhead increases in the future. Therefore, not only does this represent a unilateral federal move but Ottawa has indicated that there will be more of the same in the future. The negative implications of this transcends the impact on the provinces: it introduces a degree of economic uncertainty for the industry as well.

The second aspect of this 8 per cent levy is that it, in effect, "taxes" provincially-owned companies. Saskatchewan has already served notice on Ottawa that it will take this to the Supreme Court because in its view it contravenes Section 125 of the *BNA Act*, which states that "No Lands or Property belonging to Canada or any Province shall be liable to Taxation."

Industry impact

In the introduction to this section I noted that federal-provincial rent sharing must of necessity involve controversy because it was a zero-sum game. However, it would appear that once one takes into account the impact on the industry itself, the effect of the NEP may well be to involve Canada in a *negative-sum game*. Let me elaborate. The western industrialized world finds its economies in a rather depressed state, largely as the combined result of energy price increases and the siphoning off of purchasing power to OPEC. Almost alone among industrialized nations, Canada is self-sufficient in energy and the energy sector was providing the major engine of Canadian economic growth. The impact of the budget was clearly to clobber the energy sector, at least over the shorter term. Cash flow for the industry will remain flat (in fact decrease slightly) over 1981. This is bound to sap the dynamism from the energy sector. Even if one is in agreement with the underlying principles of Canadianization and public ownership that characterize the NEP, it is not difficult to understand the mood of the West in response to the immediate term prospect of the energy industry and jobs moving south. It is roughly equivalent to Ottawa unilaterally informing Ottawa that its auto industry has to become Canadian-owned by 1985 and leaving to Ontario the uncertainty that this would generate.

Resumé

At the outset, I asserted that Ottawa needed more revenues from energy and that much of this would likely have to be at the expense of the producing provinces. However, in my opinion the NEP goes far too far in this direction. For one thing, there no longer remain any "ground rules" to the federalism game. All of these measures are unilateral. They are not backed up by agreements. They can be changed at will and Ottawa has already indicated that it will likely revise the 8 per cent levy upwards. As W.A. Macdonald's earlier quote suggested, this provokes the unavoidable question of whether one wants to continue at a table where one's chips don't count in the game. In large measure, the medium is the message!

It is not only that the producing provinces are being forced to transfer funds to Ottawa. It is also the case that total energy revenues will fall (the negative-sum aspect) as a result of the budget, relative to what one would have expected based on the price increases alone. The latest rounds of bonus bids for exploring rights are yielding only a fraction of their former revenues. And this might only be the tip of the iceberg in terms of the short-term problems that will beset the energy sector and, therefore, all of Canada over the shorter term.

Thus, the combination of less-than-expected wellhead increases for both oil and gas, a larger Ottawa revenue grab than was expected, a detrimental short-run impact on the energy industry, and a unilateral shift of powers in the federal direction has led to a very serious crisis in this country. The Alberta response to withhold oil production and to delay approving oil sands projects serves only to heighten the tension not only between Alberta and Ottawa but between East and West. It is difficult to pinpoint which of the factors was most responsible for triggering the negative responses — probably all of them contribute a bit. The overall impact will surely be to exacerbate all aspects of federal-provincial relations, not only those identified above. For the remainder of this section I want to focus on some more specific items in the NEP that will also contribute to increasing the fiscal tensions between Ottawa and the provinces.

C. THE CANADA LANDS

Setting aside the pricing and rent-sharing aspects of the NEP, the proposal which is likely to have the most bearing on fiscal federalism is the distinction made for purposes of exploration, development and depletion between Canada Lands and provincial lands. (Basically, Canada Lands are those that fall under federal jurisdiction.) For example, depletion allowances for domestic exploration expenditures *outside* of the Canada Lands (i.e., within provincial boundaries) will be phased out, beginning in 1982. Moreover, incentive payments for exploration on provincial lands will be substantially less than those obtainable on Canada Lands, even for firms which are 100 per cent Canadian-owned. Ottawa's rationale for this differentiation is two-fold. First, exploration on the frontier is more risky and the return probably more distant. Second, the producing provinces have in place important incentives of their own, designed to foster in-province exploration and development (NEP, p. 97). There is, however, probably another reason, namely that Ottawa is not too excited about providing large incentives for exploration when a substantial return on any find will end up in provincial coffers. I can understand, but I am not in sympathy with this rationale because the implications of this decision are, in my opinion, extremely serious.

In effect, Ottawa is telling the provinces that it is up to them to provide any additional incentives in this area. Presumably they would do this via the corporate income tax route. Hence it is an incentive (and an invitation!) for the energy producing provinces to pull out of the tax collection agreements and to "patriate" their corporate income tax systems. Alberta is in the process of doing this anyway. The problem is that any changes in the provincial corporate tax system will probably *not* be limited to the energy area. Rather, the affected provinces may well utilize their tax systems as a vehicle for provincial economic development. Not only would the common allocation formula for corporate profits likely be in jeopardy, but as well Canada may face the spectre of having 10 corporate tax systems. Moreover, if corporate taxes can be used in this manner, so can personal tax systems and the Quebec approach of offering special incentives for residents' purchases of new equity issues of Quebec-based companies may become fairly widespread. In short, Canada could be opening the door to a veritable tax jungle — a beggar-my-neighbour system which will surely embody negative economic implications for resource allocation and economic growth.†

The provincial response will surely be that if Ottawa, for its own tax purposes, can discriminate on the basis of the location of economic activity, so can the provinces. I may be overly pessimistic on this issue, but it is my opinion that this provision will lead to a significant further fragmentation of the internal common market in Canada.

D. THE HERITAGE FUND

The NEP reduced substantially the present value of Alberta's Heritage Fund. In addition, the rather harsh measures directed towards the energy industry, and particularly in Alberta on the "provincial lands", means that the economic growth potential for this province has been reduced, at least in the shorter term. Thus far, as noted above, the Heritage Fund has not been used very much for pro-Alberta development. I suspect that the overall impact of the budget was such that Albertans may have second thoughts about how to allocate the resources of the fund. This is especially the case in light of the recent comments from the Maritime opposition leaders to the effect that they fear the implications of a continuation of the Heritage Fund policy of lending money to provincial governments and their agencies. (This is the golden rule principle: he who supplies the gold eventually makes the rules!) If these provinces are afraid of portfolio investment, they will be all the more fearful of direct or equity investment. But where do they suggest that the Heritage Fund *ought* to invest its money?

For both these reasons, therefore, I think that there is a distinct possibility that the Heritage Fund will be used in a much more aggressive pro-Alberta fashion in the future. As I have argued elsewhere this will not be in the long-run interests of Alberta.[9] However, it will surely be to the short-run *detriment* of provinces like Ontario and Quebec whose industries Alberta may be willing to entice West. Whatever Alberta's intentions, it is clearly the case that, at the margin, the incentives for Alberta to utilize the Heritage Fund as a vehicle for a pro-Alberta development mechanism have been increased as a result of the budget.

†Editor's Note: Canada has, in the past, had such a 'tax jungle'. For a discussion of the history of the evolution of the tax system the reader should consult 'The Tangled Tale of Taxes and Transfers' in, *Canadian Confederation at the Crossroads*, M. Walker, editor, The Fraser Institute, 1978.

This would be a most retrograde step indeed since it could lead to the very worst sort of beggar-my-neighbour federalism and elicit responses from the rest of the partners in the federation.

E. THE GAS BANK

There is an excess supply of natural gas in the West and as a result the cash flow problems of many gas producers are particularly acute. Under the NEP, the federal government will set up a Gas Bank that among other things will be prepared to purchase gas that cannot find markets from Canadian-owned and Canadian-controlled firms. On the surface, this appears to be all well and good. However, from the point of view of the West this has a particularly negative ring to it. It looks to them very much like Ottawa is taxing their resources, using some of the resulting funds to buy up excess gas at currently depressed prices, and then selling the gas later when the price is higher. Whether or not Ottawa can actually profit from this scheme will depend, among other things, on the percentage increase in the price of gas relative to the interest rate. In any event it will probably not sit well with Alberta and British Columbia who will receive royalties only on the current sale price, and not on the resale value. This is surely an area where the various participants should be able to get together and strike up a mutually acceptable agreement. Without such an agreement, the Gas Bank will clearly be viewed as yet another unwarranted federal intrusion into the provincial arena.

V. THE IMPACT ON THE REGIONS

I began this paper with an analysis of the impact of energy on the federation. It is useful to return to some of these issues, although the analysis will be very selective. The transfer required of Ontario, for example, is considerably less under the new arrangements because a much larger proportion of the funds accruing to the energy sector will find their way to Ottawa's coffers. In turns, this means lower tax rates than would be the case under the old arrangements. On the other hand, the fact that the energy industry itself appears to be reeling under the impact of the budget means that the energy spinoff in terms of jobs for

Ontarians is similarly diminished — again this is certainly true for the short run and perhaps for the long run as well.

The Atlantic region comes off fairly well under the program. The cost of paying for world-price imported oil will be blended into the cost that all Canadians pay at the pump. Ottawa has given the go-ahead for the Quebec and Maritimes gas pipeline, with a pricing system that establishes the price at the Halifax city gate at the same level as in Ontario. Given that gas is rather expensive to transport this is extremely favourable to the Atlantic region. In addition, there are several special programs amounting to over one half billion dollars over the next four years that are geared to Atlantic Canada. This may or may not imply something about the future level of equalization payments. It would seem to me that it would be difficult for the Atlantic region to argue that, in adition, they deserve more equalization payments from energy. Offsetting this is the fact that the NEP defines the offshore oil and gas finds in this region to fall under Canada Lands.

In the West, Saskatchewan comes off extremely well, relative to the other energy producing provinces. Since it has very little natural gas, it is not affected by the 8 per cent levy on operating revenues of gas companies. The 8 per cent levy does affect oil operations in the province and, as noted above, Premier Blakeney has taken exception to the fact that this will also be a levy on provincial Crown corporations. Offsetting this is the proposal whereby Ottawa will return one-half of the oil export tax on heavy oil to the provinces. Since much of Canada's heavy oil exports emanate from Saskatchewan, this is a significant increase in revenues. Moreover, the NEP includes a commitment by the Government of Canada to participate financially in a heavy crude oil upgrading plant in Saskatchewan along with changes in federal tax treatment of such plants that will enhance their viability.

Most of the negative elements I have been discussing above fall most heavily on Alberta and to a lesser extent on British Columbia. However, there are some offsetting features on the "expenditure" side of the NEP. For example, the Government of Canada will establish a special fund of $4 billion over the first part of the decade to finance a series of economic development initiatives in the four western provinces, to be chosen jointly by the two levels of government. Moreover:

> ". . . the Government of Canada will bring more than money to the table. It will examine as a matter of high priority how its trade policies could be strengthened or modified to take into account the

> need to realize the potential of the west. . . . This document has already noted the federal government's desire not to see more *oil*-based petrochemical capacity in Canada. This means concentration of future growth of this industry in western Canada, principally in Alberta. The Government of Canada will support this trend." (NEP, p. 79).

These concessions, some of them long desired by the West, have tended to be overlooked in the crossfire relating to the overall implications of the NEP.

VI. CONCLUSION

I foresee a rather bleak and fractious period ahead for federal-provincial relations on the financial front. How could it be otherwise? I have already alluded to some of the likely consequences in the key areas of preserving the integrity of the internal common market and the future role of the Heritage Fund. In 1982 the fiscal arrangements — equalization, the established program and probably the shared-cost program for welfare — come up for review. These are, in effect, federal programs and can be changed unilaterally by Ottawa. On the one hand, Ottawa's fiscal position has been improved somewhat by the NEP. On the other, the NEP represents a move toward centralization of economic and political power in Ottawa. The former might suggest that Ottawa now has more fiscal room to satisfy the perennial provincial demands for greater funds in these areas. The latter might indicate that the federal government will move in the direction of curtailing provincial powers in these areas. I do not wish to speculate on the outcome.

An Option Foregone

I want to conclude by putting forth, once again,[10] my own views as to what should have been included in the new energy package as it relates to federal-provincial revenue-sharing. This is not meant principally as an attempt to persuade — it is probably too late for this. Rather, it will put in clearer perspective some of the concerns that I have with the NEP. Underlying my approach is the assumption that Ottawa "deserves" to garner more revenues from the energy sector. A second concern relates to the issue of public ownership raised earlier in the paper. I feel strongly that Canada ought to eliminate the existing distortion that provides a substantial incentive for provincial (and federal) ownership of profit-making enterprises. Briefly put, economic activity whether undertaken in the private or public sector ought to be subject to the same tax treatment. In essence this means that "factor incomes" accruing to governments (essentially profits, interests and rents, including royalties) ought to be subject to the same tax treatment as factor income arising in the private sector. The third point underlying this approach is my belief that action on the energy front should not be perceived as arbitrary — arbitrary in the sense that it is directed against a particular industry and/or a particular region. Our federation cannot long survive under a welter of arbitrary decisions. Some principle or other must be present so that one and all know what the rules of the game are now and in the future.

The specific proposal then is that all government factor incomes be taxable by the other level of government.[11]† In practice what this would mean is that Alberta's royalties would be subject to federal taxes. So would the interest income of the Heritage Fund. However, so would the profits of Ontario's liquor monopoly, of Ontario Hydro, of Quebec Hydro, etc. On the other hand, the provinces would be able to get their share of the profits from the Bank of Canada, for example. The precise manner in which the taxing scheme would operate would be open for discussion. One obvious alternative would be to apply the present federal corporate rate of 35 per cent to the "net factor incomes" of provincial enterprises. Another approach would be to channel (implicitly) these revenues through to the individual citizens of the respective provinces and apply the federal personal tax rate to them.

This would provide Ottawa with a very substantial amount of revenue from the energy sector. In addition to any corporate tax on company profits, it would receive roughly one-third of any provincial energy-related royalties (after deducting the provincial expenses made in order to generate these revenues). The energy producing provinces could respond by saying that this violates Section 125 of the *BNA Act*. And it may well do so. But somewhere along the line this provision is going to have to be altered, and in any event it is breached in the NEP

†Editor's Note: To some extent this resolves the differences between Professors Courchene and Norrie about the usefulness of the Gainer-Powrie proposal, a variant of which Courchene is proposing and which Norrie criticizes in his paper in this volume. The taxation of provincial royalties, for example, would increase the federal share, even without a special super-normal profits tax that Norrie suggests would be inevitable.

(this is why Saskatchewan intends to take Ottawa to court). Provinces like Quebec and Ontario may object to it because they are not willing to share with Ottawa the proceeds from the export of electricity, from liquor profits, or whatever. But this would seem to me to be a very narrow view of cooperative federalism — to insist on one's own rights while allowing Ottawa to run over those of others.

As a *quid quo pro* the provinces would probably be given more responsibility for pricing and managing their resources. The implications for the energy industry under this scheme would essentially be neutral. That is, within this framework, Canada could move to tax the energy sector more heavily than it did prior to the budget if it so wished. It could engage in nationalization if it wanted, etc.

My purpose in focusing on this proposal is not to argue that it is necessarily airtight. Nor do I want to minimize the difficulties that would arise — e.g. how does one distinguish a factor income from a tax? Rather, it is to argue that there are alternative approaches to the NEP which could also generate a large federal cash flow from energy. More importantly, they can be built upon a *principle* (in this case namely that factor incomes accruing to governments be taxed in the same manner as factor incomes accruing to individuals) that would probably be accepted as equitable by most Canadians (and, hopefully by some provinces as well). In addition, while the major impact would in the current context be on the energy sector, the approach would apply equally to *all provinces and to Ottawa as well.* It seems to me that it is this lack of any sort of guiding principle underlying the NEP and, therefore, the likelihood of increased arbitrariness in the future that is contributing as much as the substance of the energy policy itself to the current malaise besetting federalism. I am convinced Canadians as individuals and as residents of particular provinces are not as far apart on energy matters as the present crisis would lead us to believe. I submit this proposal as one of the range of options that at the same time may offer an acceptable compromise on the energy front and preserve the concept of fair play that is so essential to the vitality and economic integrity of our federalism. Unfortunately, I feel that the National Energy Program does neither.

FOOTNOTES

1 Much of this section is taken from an article by Thomas J. Courchene and James R. Melvin, "Energy Revenues and Consequences for the Rest of Canada," *Canadian Public Policy/Analyse de Politique* VI, Special Issue, 1980, pp. 192-204.

2 "Energy and Equalization" in *Energy Policy for the 1980's: An Economic Analysis* [Toronto: Ontario Economic Council, 1980].

3 It is the case, however, that the oil import compensation payments will disappear if and when Canada goes to the world price of energy. In this sense they are an "indirect" expenditure, based on Ottawa's decision to hold down the domestic price of energy.

4 T.J. Courchene, "Energy and Equalization" *op. cit.*

5 Note that the equalization system is financed from Ottawa's consolidated revenue fund. Rich provinces do *not* contribute directly to the financing of the program.

6 F. Flatters and D. Purvis, "Ontario: Between Alberta and the Deep Blue Sea?" forthcoming in an Ontario Economic Council Conference volume on supply-side economics.

7 W.A. Macdonald, Q.C., "Notes for Prentice-Hall Budget Seminar," October 29, 1980, mimeo.

8 This neglects the "industry" side of things, which will be dealt with later.

9 Courchene and Melvin, *op. cit.*

10 Thomas J. Courchene, "The Issue is Not Price, It's How to Share the Money," *Globe and Mail*, October 28, 1980, p. 7. The heart of the proposal, namely the taxing of factor incomes accruing to governments, is adapted from a paper by Professors W. Gainer and T. Powrie of the University of Alberta, "Public Revenue from Canadian Crude Petroleum Production," *Canadian Public Policy*, I, 1 (1975), pp. 1-12.

11 This concept is really not very different from that intended in 1974. By ruling that provincial royalties would not be deductible by companies for federal income tax purposes the federal government implicitly was taxing these royalties. If royalties would be deductible, the provinces would clearly increase them sufficiently so that they would crowd out federal income taxes. Ottawa's problems arose when it decided to provide very generous deductions for the energy industry, so much so that in one recent year a major multinational paid no corporate tax. But the principle involved when not allowing a deduction for royalties is a close relative of my proposal. I should note that under my scheme, royalties *would* be deductible and, therefore, they would probably become higher. But Ottawa would share in the increased revenues.

Chapter 5

The National Energy Program: A Western Perspective

KENNETH H. NORRIE
Department of Economics
University of Alberta

THE AUTHOR

KENNETH H. NORRIE, an Associate Professor at the University of Alberta in Edmonton and Visiting Associate Professor (1979/80) at Queen's University, Kingston, Ontario, was born in 1946 in Saskatchewan. He received his B.A. (Honours) in 1966 from the University of Saskatchewan, his M.Phil. in 1969 and his Ph.D. in 1971 from Yale University, New Haven, Connecticut.

Professor Norrie teaches Introductory Economics, Intermediate Macroeconomics, Economic Development, Canadian Economic Development, Economics of the Prairie Region and Regional Economics. He is a former member of the Editorial Board of the *Canadian Journal of Economics.*

Numerous articles and papers by Professor Norrie have appeared in the *Canadian Journal of Economics*, *Journal of Economic History*, *Canadian Public Policy/Analyse de Politiques*, *Agricultural History*, *Canadian Papers in Rural History*, *Canadian Journal of Political Science*, and the *Journal of Canadian Studies*. He has also prepared studies for and presented papers to the Economic Council of Canada, the Institute of Intergovernmental Relations, and the Science Council of Canada. He was a contributing author to the Fraser Institute publication *Privatization: Theory and Practice*.

The National Energy Program: A Western Perspective*

KENNETH H. NORRIE

Department of Economics
University of Alberta

I. INTRODUCTION

While this paper offers some general comments on the economy-wide implications of the National Energy Program (NEP), most of the attention is devoted to its regional features. I have taken this perspective because there is a lamentable tendency outside of the region to underestimate the extent of the opposition to the NEP in the West, and as a result to adopt a much too sanguine view of Canada's energy future. What follows then is an attempt to elaborate on this Western position and to assess what it might mean for the nation more generally.

The main features of the NEP are summarized elsewhere in this volume, and need not be repeated here. The paper proceeds by way of discussing five different points, each of which forms a separate section below. It argues first that the case for higher oil prices in Canada is a convincing one, and then that the case against them is not. The third point is that the partitioning of petroleum revenue as presented in the NEP document is misleading. The federal share is actually larger than the document indicates. I also argue that the measures proposed will not alter the respective shares much, but will validate the change in them that took place in 1973. Section four discusses what the shares should be and concludes that the only logical division is one that does not compromise the provincial ownership of resources. The final section comments on the possibility of, and results from, a continuing political deadlock in the energy issue.

*I wish to acknowledge discussions with Bruce Wilkinson and especially Brian Scarfe during the preparation of this paper.

II. THE CASE FOR HIGHER ENERGY PRICES

The case for higher energy prices on economic efficiency grounds is one of the propositions about which most economists agree. The static allocative losses occur on both the demand and the supply side, as has been clearly demonstrated in Campbell Watkins' essay in this volume.

Watkins' calculations show that the deadweight loss associated with the NEP's lower-than-world-price provisions will amount to $3.4 billion per year during 1984. Helliwell (1980) also provides evidence of substantial efficiency losses stemming, interestingly enough, almost entirely from the natural gas side. Clearly then, the static allocative costs of maintaining petroleum product prices artificially low are substantial and, taken in conjunction with other less tangible ones (Watkins, 1980, 10-14) provide a convincing case in favour of abandoning this particular aspect of the NEP.

III. THE CASE AGAINST WORLD OIL PRICES

If the efficiency loss is so large and so apparent, it might be asked, why does the government choose to continue the policy? There are several arguments typically advanced to defend this position. The first is the belief that the world price is somehow an artificial one, and that the Canadian price need not necessarily bear any relationship to it. One can do no better than quote from the NEP itself on this (p. 27):

> "World oil prices are arbitrary and artificial. They do not reflect conditions of competitive supply and demand, nor the costs of production in Canada or other countries. The Government is determined that the price of Canadian oil will not be linked to world oil prices, but rather will be "made-in-Canada" — determined on the basis of Canadian circumstances, and the needs of Canada's economy."

They are temporarily high†

The argument makes no economic sense of course.[1] Each barrel of oil consumed in Canada means one less available for export at world prices, or one more purchased from abroad, again at world prices. In either case the relevant opportunity cost of Canadian consumption

†Editor's Note: Refer to C. Watkins' paper in this volume.

is the world, or at least the Chicago, price. It may have made sense to divorce Canadian prices from world levels in the early stages when it was unclear how stable the OPEC cartel would prove to be, recognizing that there would have been real economic costs to adjusting to a transitory phenomenon. But now that the cartel has proven itself to be as durable as it has, and, thus, that there is little likelihood of oil prices falling significantly, this position has ceased to have any relevance.

Low income earners are too hard hit by price increases

The second argument that one encounters is that higher energy prices will affect low income earners disproportionately. The most recent evidence we have on this, however, suggests just the opposite. Oil price subsidies appear to benefit the rich both absolutely and proportionately (Waverman 1980). In addition, even if the reverse were true, or even if a smaller proportionate effect were still judged serious, there are other more efficient ways through the tax system to shield the poor from energy price increases. Subsidizing them as energy consumers rather than as taxpayers is simply perverse.

Higher prices only mean windfalls to foreigners and higher inflation rates

T.A. Wilson (1980) argues against rapid adjustment to world oil prices, under current institutional arrangements as he stresses, on grounds that this would provide an unduly large windfall gain to foreigners and would increase inflationary expectations significantly, thereby worsening the inflation-unemployment trade-off. On the first issue, Scarfe and Wilkinson (1980) estimate that a $1 increase in oil prices results in increased payments to foreigners of at least 21 cents. For gas and oil taken together, this figure would be somewhat less. Wilson goes on to argue that this loss is greater than the micro-efficiency gain, so that Canadians are actually worse off as a result. Clearly though, as these and other writers point out,[2] this is really a case for implementing taxation or other measures to capture as much of this transfer as is economically efficient, rather than a case for keeping prices low. In this respect, the moves contained in the NEP towards encouraging greater Canadian ownership of the industry are useful.

The point regarding the general inflationary implications of a price rise is more difficult to deal with. We are dealing with a relative price increase, so people "should not" incorporate these into their inflation estimates. It seems pretty clear that they do though, and, thus, that the issue must be raised. Three points can be made on this. First, although there is no real consensus on the point, it seems plausible to suggest that gradual increases in oil prices have a larger impact on inflationary expectations than a sudden, once-and-for-all move. Hence, something may be gained by more, as opposed to less, rapid adjustment to world price levels. Second, even the Alberta position on pricing represents a phased-in approach to world prices, albeit a more rapid one, and that is all that is being advocated here. Finally, this position ignores the supply side effects of higher energy prices. If keeping prices low now does adversely affect our chances of moving towards greater self-sufficiency, as is claimed, then the eventual adjustment in price we face may be very great indeed.

Lower oil prices provide a competitive edge

If it is often posited that Canada needs lower oil prices in order to give its industry a competitive edge in world markets. Moreover, this opinion persists in spite of compelling evidence to the contrary. For example, energy costs are typically not a significant enough component of total manufacturing costs for a subsidy to make much overall difference, especially when factor substitution possibilities are recognized (Waverman, 1980).[3] In total, energy use accounts for only about 5 per cent of industrial costs. Even to the extent energy costs are significant and lower oil prices do provide a significant benefit, is it clear that we wish to subsidize energy intensive industries disproportionately? Especially when we realize that the large firms in the petroleum and chemical products industries are largely foreign-owned. Will this not create an even worse adjustment problem later as Canadian fuel prices move more quickly to world levels?

The Dutch disease

A variant of this argument which also leads to concern over the fate of Ontario industry is the so-called "Dutch disease" (Flatters and Purvis, 1980). The proposition here is that a natural resources export boom plus the associated capital flows drive up the exchange rate to a point where domestic manufactured goods are no longer competitive. In addition, the large public sector revenues generated in Holland were allegedly spent largely on domestic services, pushing up these prices and, thus, the costs of the manufacturing sector even further. The end result is deindustrialization.

The question then is whether Canada, and specifically Ontario manufacturing, would contact the Dutch disease if Canada were to move to world oil prices. The answer to this is surely not, an opinion shared by Flatters and Purvis it should be noted (p. 28). A rise in price would gradually reduce our dependence on imported oil, which would tend to strengthen the Canadian dollar all else being equal. But it is difficult to imagine that the magnitudes involved here could have any significant impact on the overall balance. In addition, to the extent that 30 per cent of any additional revenues Alberta would receive would go directly to the Heritage Savings Trust Fund, and that both levels of government are committed to plowing at least a portion of the returns back into energy sector investments, the public sector wage and price inflation effect should not be any more significant than it already has been.

Sharing the pie problems

The most substantial issue in the debate arises from the fact that under current institutional arrangements energy price increases lead to substantial income redistributions within Canada.[4] The producing provinces, primarily Alberta, receive large windfall gains by virtue of their ownership position. Seven of the ten provinces produce no oil or gas, but pay the higher price. Six of these receive equalization payments to offset part of this, but Ontario is specifically excluded. The federal government pays the increased equalization grants out of general revenues, with consequent budgetary deterioration at great political cost. More than anything else perhaps, it is this problem of the internal distribution of the revenues that has prevented the move to a more rational pricing system.

The concern over internal distribution has both an efficiency and an equity side. The latter is discussed in the next two sections. The efficiency issue centres on the concept of fiscal-induced migration. The argument proceeds as follows.[5] Any rise in the price of petroleum products will generate a substantial amount of extra public sector revenue for Alberta. That province will, in turn, use at least a portion of it to subsidize the consumption of public goods and services by provincial residents. This means that an individual in Alberta with the same wage as his Ontario counterpart is actually better off. The Ontario worker, realizing this, will migrate to Alberta, driving down the marginal product of labour there and raising it in Ontario. The migrant is, in effect, trading off a lower private return for access to cheaper public goods. This process will then continue until the last worker to move sacrifices just enough in terms of wage rates to exactly offset the expected fiscal gain. From society's point of view the end result is inefficient since the output gained by adding the worker to the Alberta labour force is less than that foregone by him leaving the original one.

The question that arises then is how, assuming away any changes in the revenue sharing schemes, this efficiency loss compares to the production and consumption losses discussed above. To our knowledge no one has attempted this type of calculation rigorously as yet. Flatters and Purvis (1980) argue that the former likely "swamps" the latter (p. 18) and that oil price increases under current arrangements are likely to lead to "tremendous waste" (p. 23). But is this so obvious? While this is not the place to debate this issue fully, some general points can be raised.[6] It must be recognized first of all that it is government expenditure rather than revenue that is relevant to the argument. Thirty per cent of Alberta's energy revenues go automatically into the Heritage Savings Trust Fund, and recently at least the government has run a large budget surplus as well. Thus not all natural resource revenues should be included when judging the likelihood of fiscal migration. Indeed, to the extent that some of the Heritage Fund has been lent to other provincial governments, and has allowed them to provide public goods without raising taxes immediately, the effect is in the other direction. But it is still true that there are significant fiscal advantages to residing in Alberta, so the issue needs to be confronted more directly.

One might query two of the assumptions implicit in the notion. It assumes first of all that migration is actually responsive to fiscal differences, something which is far from clearly established as yet.[7] It also assumes that there is no capitalization of fiscal advantages into land prices. If land were in perfectly inelastic supply for example, any fiscal advantage would be fully offset by higher land costs. A potential migrant would literally have to buy his tax saving, and the net advantage of the move would be zero. The greater the long run elasticity of serviced land is of course, the less effective is this offset mechanism. It certainly is true currently that housing prices in Edmonton and Calgary are relatively high, and some have interpreted this as a sign that resource revenues are at least imperfectly capitalized. Others, however, view it as an adjustment phenomenon resulting from an inelastic short run land supply. Until the evidence is in on this, it must be left as a conjecture.

Another problem with the argument is that wages in Alberta have not fallen relative to other areas, quite the contrary in fact. This could suggest that any interregional reallocation of labour required by the relative expansion of the energy sector over the last decade has proceeded only slowly and imperfectly. If there are costs to having the labour market only imperfectly adjusting over time, as there surely are, and if fiscal incentives are at least drawing workers in the right direction, then perhaps in at least this adjustment phase they provide a new benefit to society. We may still eventually overshoot and end up with too much westward migration and the efficiency loss this implies, but the net effect discounted over time is now uncertain. To repeat, this is not to suggest that this is necessarily true; the calculations are yet to be made. It simply argues that the fiscal-induced migration argument is not necessarily as certain as the deadweight losses discussed above.

In fairness to its proponents, the fiscal-induced migration argument is really offered as a case for altering the way natural resource revenues are distributed within Canada, rather than for maintaining artificially low oil prices. Given this lead then, we can move on to discuss the sharing arrangements that are proposed in the NEP.

IV. REVENUE SHARES — PRESENT AND PROPOSED

Shares depend on definition of total pie

There are two simple questions to be raised in connection with revenue sharing. What are the respective shares to be under the NEP, and what should they be? Unfortunately, neither has a simple answer. We deal with the first question here and the second one in the following section. The response to the first query is that it depends how one defines revenue shares. There are many separate variants possible.[8] One is simply to note that the consumer price (the so-called "blended" price) is to rise by $14.30 between September, 1980 and December, 1983. Of this, $8.30 or 58 per cent represents the increase in the Petroleum Compensation Charge (NEP p. 30). Of the $1.35 per Mcf rise in the price of natural gas over the same period, 75¢ or 56 per cent represents the yield of the natural gas tax. Under this definition, the federal government is taking more than half of the incremental revenue.

The NEP share definitions

These calculations are incomplete, however, since they assume both levies can be passed forward completely, and they ignore a host of other taxes and subsidies. Table I presents a variety of revenue shares, based on the breakdown of estimated revenues from oil and gas production as presented in the NEP publication (p. 108). Rows 1 to 3 give the estimated revenue in 1980 and the distribution of the total and of the public sector component. Rows 4 through 6 present the same information for 1983. The federal share of total revenues almost exactly doubles from 14 per cent in 1980 to 27.5 per cent in 1983. Its share of public sector revenue goes up from nearly 23 per cent to over 40 per cent. The portion of the increment that the federal government is to receive is higher of course (rows 7 to 9), being over 43 per cent of the total increment and 56.3 per cent of the public sector increment.[9] By the NEP's own calculations then, the average federal share doubles under either definition by imposing marginal tax rates of either 43 per cent or 56 per cent.

Some suspicious calculations

The calculations reported in the last paragraph are suspect however, since they are based on a rather special definition of what constitutes the federal share. Specifically, they exclude all but $1 billion of Petroleum Compensation Charge receipts.[10] The report has excluded any revenues the federal government raises which it turns over to consumers. The $1 billion is included only because it represents an excess of estimated collections over expenditures under the subsidy program on imported oil. In effect, revenue raised under the Petroleum Compensation Charge only counts as federal revenue in the document if it is surplus to import subsidy requirements and thus available for other purposes.

It might be argued, however, that the decision to continue to subsidize imported oil was taken consciously by the federal government, and is in effect an expenditure decision which should be treated as such. To the extent that it is financed through a petroleum levy then, this should be treated as federal revenue, even if all the government actually does is make two offsetting accounting moves. If it chose to discontinue the subsidy but retain the tax, federal net revenues would clearly rise, and by their own accounting would be included. But this procedure admits the separation of the revenue and expenditure

TABLE I
ESTIMATED REVENUES FROM OIL AND GAS PRODUCTION, 1980-1983

	Federal	Industry	Provinces
1. Net Revenue, 1980 ($ billion)	2.2	6.1	7.4
2. Percent Distribution	14.0	38.9	47.1
3. Percent Distribution of Public Sector Revenue	22.9	—	77.1
4. Net Revenue, 1983 ($ billion)	8.0	9.2	11.9
5. Percent Distribution	27.5	31.6	40.9
6. Percent Distribution of Public Sector Revenue	40.2	—	59.8
7. Change in Net Revenues, 1980-83 ($ billion)	5.8	3.1	4.5
8. Percent Share of Incremental Revenue	43.3	23.1	33.6
9. Percent Share of Incremental Public Sector Revenue	56.3	—	43.7
10. Revenue in 1983 including PCC ($ billion)	10.2	9.2	11.9
11. Percent Distribution	32.5	29.4	38.0
12. Percent Distribution of Public Sector Revenue	46.2	—	53.8
13. Change in Revenue including PCC, 1980-83 ($ billion)	8.0	3.1	4.5
14. Percent Share of Incremental Revenue	51.3	19.9	28.8
15. Percent Share of Incremental Public Sector Revenue	64.0	—	36.0
16. Revenue in 1980 including price subsidy to consumers allocated to federal ($ billion)	17.7	6.1	7.4
17. Percent Distribution	56.7	19.6	23.7
18. Percent Distribution of Public Sector Revenue	70.5	—	29.5
19. Revenue in 1983 with estimated price subsidy allocated to Federal and World Price equal to $45.80	20.3	9.2	11.9
20. Percent Distribution	49.0	22.2	28.7
21. Percent Distribution of Public Sector Revenue	63.0	—	37.0
22. As in Row 19, but with World Price equal to $50.00	23.4	9.2	11.9
23. Percent Distribution	52.6	20.7	26.7
24. Percent Distribution of Public Sector Revenue	66.3	—	33.7
25. Change in Revenue, 1980-83 (Row 19 - Row 16)	2.6	3.1	4.5
26. Percent Share of Incremental Revenue	25.6	30.4	44.1

TABLE I (Continued)
ESTIMATED REVENUES FROM OIL AND GAS PRODUCTION, 1980-1983

	Federal	Industry	Provinces
27. Percent Share of Incremental Public Sector Revenue	36.6	—	63.4
28. Change in Revenue, 1980-83 (Row 22 - Row 16)	5.7	3.1	4.5
29. Percent Share of Incremental Revenue	42.9	23.3	33.8
30. Percent Share of Incremental Public Sector Revenue	55.9	—	44.1
31. Percent Distribution in 1980, Allowing 25% of Price Subsidy to Provinces	44.3	19.6	36.1
32. Percent Distribution of Public Sector Revenues	55.1	—	44.9
33. Percent Distribution in 1983 for World Price equals $45.80, allowing 25% of price subsidy to provinces	42.9	22.2	34.8
34. Percent Distribution of Public Sector Revenue	55.2	—	44.8

Source: Calculations based on The National Energy Program, Canada, Energy, Mines and Resources (1980) p. 108 plus discussion in text.

process, and thus requires including total Petroleum Compensation Charges in the federal share.

Why the NEP is said to be confiscatory

Wilkinson (1980) estimates that an additional $2.2 billion should be included in total federal revenue for 1983.[11] Rows 10 through 12 of the Table give total revenue and its distribution with this included, and rows 13 through 15 perform the marginal calculations. The federal share rises from 14 per cent in 1980 to 32.5 per cent by this definition, and to 46.2 per cent of the public sector revenue. The marginal rates implied by this are significantly higher, being over one-half of the increase in total revenue and nearly two-thirds of the increase in public sector revenue. It is these type of figures that have led some to label the NEP as confiscatory (e.g. Scarfe, 1981). In order to increase its average take to about one-half, Ottawa appears to be ready to appropriate nearly two-thirds of all public sector revenues over the next three years. The inequity is said to be in the discrepancy between its traditional average share of this rent[12] and the drastically higher marginal rates now.

Uncounted taxes and hidden subsidies

However, the same logic that called for including Petroleum Compensation Charges in the federal share also requires that the subsidy to consumers arising from keeping Canadian oil prices below the world level be counted as part of the federal share. Doing this changes the interpretation of the figures somewhat. If this amount were collected as an excise tax on oil and gas consumption and then returned to consumers, it would be no different than the Petroleum Compensation Charge and would be included. The fact that the federal government chooses to short circuit this by simply holding energy prices down instead changes nothing in principle. An appropriate accounting for shares should obviously include this tax and transfer arrangement.

An appropriately calculated federal share

Rows 16 to 18 show the total revenues and the distribution of revenues in 1980 allowing for a price subsidy of $14.5 billion[13] allocated entirely to the federal share. By this calculation, the federal government in 1980 was receiving 56.7 per cent of total revenues, and over 70 per cent of the public sector revenues. In other words, the marginal rate that they have imposed on incremental revenues to 1983 is not at all out of line with the average rate that they began with. Indeed, to the extent that the blended oil price approaches the world price, thereby reducing the subsidy, the federal share will actually fall by 1983. This is illustrated in rows 19 to 21, where it is assumed that the world price in 1983 is equal to the oil sands reference price for that year of $45.80. The federal share of total revenues falls from 56.7 per cent to 49 per cent, and of public sector revenues from 70.5 per cent to 63 per cent. Rows 22 to 24 show the same calculations for a world oil price of $50. In that event the consumer subsidy is higher and the federal share in 1983 is only slightly lower.

The point being made here can perhaps be seen more clearly by looking at rows 25 through 30, where the marginal changes from 1980 to 1983 are given for the two world price assumptions. There it is shown that the federal government appropriates 25.5 per cent of total or 36.6 per cent of public sector revenues, well below the incremental share shown in rows 14 and 15 where the consumer price subsidy is excluded. The explanation for this is found by comparing row 25 to row 13. Total public sector revenues have fallen as a result of the lower consumer subsidy implicit in using the 1983 oil sands reference price as the world price, and all of this comes at the expense of federal revenues by assumption. Thus, even though the federal government gains disproportionately from the fact that the blended price is moving up faster than the wellhead price, by the assumptions employed here it loses even more by virtue of no longer subsidizing consumers to the same extent. Its actual revenues in hand will have increased over the period of course, so in a strict budgetary sense its position will have improved. This point holds, of course, even if part of the consumer subsidy is allocated to the producing provinces, as can be seen in rows 31 to 34. The federal share falls to 55 per cent from 70 per cent by this measure and remains at that level to 1983.

Industry share calculations

There are numerous problems with even these latter calculations though. The industry share reported is a gross payment rather than one net of the costs of exploring for and producing the oil and gas. Ignoring the industry share completely however, as was done when looking only at the distribution of incremental public sector revenue, misses any rent that the companies might be able to appropriate. Since the time lag between expenditures and eventual revenues can be considerable, the stream of rents over time should be capitalized into a present value rather than looked at for individual years. Finally, the economic waste is ignored above. The shares were allocated over actual revenue generated, and then over actual revenue plus the consumer subsidy. Potential rent includes these plus the deadweight efficiency losses discussed in section II.

Helliwell (1980) presents some estimates of the distribution of rents that are free from these problems. Some calculations based on these are presented in Table II.[14] As a comparison, the results for both the federal budget and for what would have happened if the July, 1980 Alberta pricing proposals were accepted are presented. Rows 1 and 5 show the distribution of the revenues actually generated, and as such correspond most closely to row 11 of Table I except, as noted, the industry share is now revenue after costs, including opportunity costs, are deducted. The federal share here is 26.2 per cent, compared to 64.8 per cent for the provinces and 9 per cent for the industry. The Alberta proposal, by contrast would have given more to the industry at the expense of the federal share. The provincial portion is nearly identical in either case. Rows 2 and 6 divide actual public sector revenues between levels of government. The federal share is nearly 30 per cent under the budget, but only 15.4 per cent under the Alberta proposals. The federal share is lower than in row 12 of Table I partly because the Helliwell model includes the period prior to 1973 when federal rent collection efforts were minimal, and partly because he appears to define the federal revenues net of import compensation payments[15] whereas Table I does not.

Rows 3 and 7 allocate the actual rent available among consumers, producers and governments for each of the pricing proposals. The extent of the subsidy to consumers is clearly evident here — over 42 per cent of the rents under the NEP proposal, and close to 30 per cent even under the Alberta scheme. These remain in the latter case since the period after 1973 is included in the calculation, and because as noted earlier Alberta's final price is still well short of world levels. If the rents to consumers are included in the federal share, as they are in row 17 of Table I for instance, this rises to 57.3 per cent compared to 37.2 per cent under the Alberta plan. Allocating one-quarter of the consumer subsidy to the producing provinces as in row 32 of Table I changes these figures to 49.4 per cent and 30.0 per cent respectively.

Perhaps the most interesting aspect of the Helliwell numbers, however, comes from comparing rows 4 and 8. This represents the allocation of potential economic rent, i.e., rent actually captured either as revenues or as subsidized prices plus that wasted through inappropriate pricing. Row 4 shows the rent dissipation to amount to over 20 per cent for the NEP program, but only 7.8 per cent under the Alberta proposals.[16] Surely no clearer case for a more efficient pricing scheme could be made. Canadians are clearly not being well served by political leaders who will allow economic losses of this magnitude to occur simply because they cannot reach agreement on a revenue sharing scheme.

V. WHAT SHOULD THE REVENUE SHARES BE?

The previous section showed that there are a variety of ways to interpret the notion of a revenue share, and thus a wide range of empirical estimates of them. Perhaps the most consistent conclusion to come out of the discussion in the preceding section is that the federal share was already high in 1980, higher than is commonly supposed once the consumer price subsidy is taken into account, but that unless world oil prices rise significantly faster than the scheduled rise in the Canadian blended price the NEP will have little marginal effect on the shares. Its main effect will be to reallocate the manner in which Ottawa receives its share, replacing subsidies to consumers by actual revenues.

Why is there such a fuss?

There are two different conclusions that could be drawn from this. The first is that if the marginal effect of the NEP is so slight (again, assuming no increasing wedge between world and Canadian blended oil prices), why all the fuss?

An alternative construction would run as follows. It is the federal share in 1980 that is far too large. The comparison that needs to be made is between the shares in 1972 and those in 1980. The price freeze and the export tax after 1972 served to appropriate an unwarranted amount of the economic rent to Ottawa. This may have been tolerable as a short run strategy, but it is clearly not in the longer run. Now that there is an increased willingness to let Canadian prices rise, sharing arrangements in place would have moved us back toward (but not necessarily returning to) the pre-1973 shares. Just as this was beginning to happen though, the NEP was instituted so as to preserve the post-1973 distribution. Thus the fault with the NEP is not that it makes significant new inroads into provincial resource revenue, but rather that it perpetuates a revenue division that was the by-product of an allegedly short term policy reaction. The producing provinces are not asking for a greater share then, but instead a return to that which traditionally was considered rightfully theirs.

In order to evaluate this latter position, one obviously needs an answer to the question, 'How much of a federal share is "too much"?' Are there grounds for arguing that the 1972 shares, and the taxation arrangements then in place to capture future rents, are superior to the 1980 ones? Or is some position in between even more desirable?

Defining a correct federal share

There are two basic positions on this from which a "correct" federal share might logically follow. The first is to accept that provincial governments own the natural resources and that under the Constitution one level of government cannot tax another. In this case, the "correct" share is whatever the producing province deems it to be. This would appear to be the position of the Alberta government, for example, when it insists as it does, that it is the principle of provincial ownership that is at stake rather than a squabble over dollars.

The obvious question that arises then is why a producing province might agree to transfer anything at all, as indeed Alberta has clearly been willing to do. One reason is simply the notion of sharing that is built into a federation. This could be based on simple generosity —provinces fortunate enough to have bouyant economies help those that do not. Or it could be based on a more calculating, insurance motive — the province does not know when it might require economic assistance itself. The other factor is that the province may just wish to avoid the costs to itself of any fiscal-induced migration it sees resulting otherwise. In other words, given that a province cannot control migration flows, it might pay it to bribe residents of other provinces not to come. Any transfer involved leaves those already in Alberta better off than they would be without the transfer, but with the migration. Obviously this motive is weaker the less responsive interprovincial migration is to fiscal differences.

An alternative position might start by recognizing that petroleum revenues are different and cause special problems by virtue of being publicly owned to such a great extent. If mineral rights had gone with land titles after 1888, as opposed to being reserved for the Crown, the economic rent would accrue to the private sector in the first instance, and the federal government would have a well-established claim on it through traditional taxation measures. The obvious suggestion then is that the "correct" federal share is precisely that amount that it would receive if the resources were privately owned. This is the much discussed Gainer-Powrie (1975) recommendation of course. The parties involved would agree to suspend (or ignore) that section of the *BNA Act*, and the producing provinces would pay "taxes" or "special payments" to the federal government on the returns they derive from natural resource production.[17]

While the principle involved in the Gainer-Powrie proposal is clear, the taxation rate implied by it is not. Powrie (1980) suggests that the relevant range is from 14.5 per cent (the per cent that total federal taxes were of GNP in 1978) to 36 per cent (the federal tax on corporate income after provincial tax credit). The earlier Gainer-Powrie paper used 30 per cent as an illustration, and that has increasingly been used to evaluate actual federal shares (Scarfe, 1981). By this standard, the federal shares under the NEP as given in Table II are clearly too high. Ottawa appears to be using the constitutional ambiguity over resource control[18] to collect a larger share than they would have if Alberta had sold off all its mineral rights by auction at the time of the transfer in 1930.

This conclusion does not necessarily follow though. For one thing, the 36 per cent ceiling ignores the fact that under private ownership the federal government would also be collecting personal income tax on dividends. Assuming a 25 per cent tax rate on these and a 30 per cent corporate tax, the federal share comes to 47.5 per cent which is much closer to the current shares. Presumably though, this would be levied on revenues net of provincial infrastructure and administrative expenditures, so the effective tax rate would be less. In addition, the government would have almost certainly imposed a "super profits" tax of some sort after 1973, given the magnitude of the revenues that were being earned. Alberta itself did precisely this at the time when it scrapped the existing contractual arrangements with the companies, and replaced them with a much higher royalty rate. Saskatchewan and British Columbia likewise imposed extra taxes on natural resource industries. Given this, it seems impossible to settle on one unique rate that the federal government would have been earning under private resource ownership. As appealing as the Gainer-Powrie notion is in principle, it does not seem to be an appropriate criterion to use to judge taxation levels implied by the NEP.[19]

By implication then we are back to the first of the two positions. The "correct" federal share is the maximum amount that the producing provinces are willing to cede, presumably in negotiation with the federal government. Arguing anything else amounts to denying the basic concept of ownership and property rights. We may rue the 1867 decision to grant ownership to the provinces rather than the central government,[20] but it was taken and it would be grossly unfair to go back on this now. It is then up to the governments of the producing provinces to convince their respective electorates as to what they perceive an appropriate share to be, and it is clearly in the interests of the other jurisdictions to try to make the portion distributed externally as high as possible. Unfortunately perhaps, there does not appear to be any other logical way to answer the question posed in the heading to this section.

TABLE II
SHARES OF PRESENT VALUE OF ECONOMICS RENTS FROM OIL AND GAS PRODUCTION

	Industry	Consumers	Waste	Federal	Provinces
Federal Budget					
1. Percent Share of Actual Revenue	9.0	—	—	26.2	64.8
2. Percent Share of Public Sector Revenue	—	—	—	28.7	71.2
3. Percent Share of Actual Economic Rent	5.2	42.2	—	15.1	37.5
4. Percent Share of Potential Economic Rent	4.1	33.4	20.9	12.0	29.6
Alberta Pricing Proposals					
5. Percent Share of Actual Revenue	21.6	—	—	12.1	66.3
6. Percent Share of Public Sector Revenue	—	—	—	15.4	84.6
7. Percent Share of Actual Economic Rent	15.5	28.6	—	8.6	47.4
8. Percent Share of Potential Economic Rent	14.3	26.4	7.8	7.9	43.7

Source: Calculated from Helliwell (1980) Table I.

VI. CONCLUSION

The main conclusions of the paper can be summarized very briefly. There is a convincing economic efficiency case for moving Canadian oil and gas prices towards world levels at a faster rate than is currently proposed, while the arguments typically advanced to oppose this are less persuasive. It was also suggested that the debate surrounding the impost of the NEP is misleading. The new arrangements will not likely alter the overall shares very much at all. The issue rather is whether the current federal share, which the NEP will largely preserve, is too high. The answer to this, it was argued, comes down to saying that it is if the producing provinces feel that it is. This position is the logical implication of taking ownership rights seriously, and there seems to be no convincing case for suspending these for petroleum resources solely.

The stalemate

One final point needs to be raised in concluding. What happens, it might be asked, if the various governments involved cannot agree on a revenue share, as is the case currently? The federal government then uses its general taxing powers and its control over interprovincial and international trade to attempt to impose its own scheme. The province responds by appealing to its ownership position and attempts to force the issue its way. The end result is stalemate and significant economic losses, with Canadians as a whole being the real losers, some more than others perhaps.

We are already seeing manifestations of this. The Alberta production cutbacks are to begin shortly, forcing the federal government to replace Alberta oil with expensive off-shore oil. Exploration activity is falling off, and rigs are leaving for the more lucrative and less unsettled U.S. plays. Oil sands and heavy oil projects are stalled because of the present political uncertainties, and it seems inevitable that some "make-work" type projects will be directed toward these communities. The federal government meanwhile is offering increasingly attractive incentives for exploration and development of Canada Lands (i.e., those under federal control) without presenting convincing evidence that this is consistent with the socially optimal sequence of development. The ultimate costs of these and other actions could be huge, making the current efficiency losses small by comparison. Resolution of the present impasse is, therefore, imperative.

Who should yield? From the discussion above it is obvious that I feel the federal government should on the crucial point of ownership. One only needs to read the statements made by Alberta politicians over the last seven years to realize just how important this is to them and apparently their electorate. It is also clear that the federal government has consistently failed to appreciate this. In my opinion, the Lougheed government is prepared to remain firm on its position at almost any cost. It is also my view that with the ownership question settled, this same government would be quite open to discussing ways in which all economic rents from all resources could be efficiently and equitably shared among Canadians. The next move rests with Ottawa. There are great economic gains to be had from making it a conciliatory one. Any other kind, such as a pre-emptive move on oil sands, would certainly have disastrous consequences.

FOOTNOTES

1 There is an interesting anomoly in the NEP. After rejecting world prices for conventional crude oil on the grounds cited in the text, it indicates on the next page (p. 25) that the price for synthetic crude oil will be $38 per barrel escalated by the Consumer Price Index, or the international price, whichever is less. In other words, the international price is only relevant as long as it is above the Canadian one. The logic of a price administered for "Canadian needs" however would seem to require symmetric treatment on either side of the international rate.

2 See also Flatters and Purvis (1980) and Waverman (1980).

3 It should be noted that Ontario energy prices were higher than world prices under the old National Oil Policy, yet this never became a major factor in productivity discussions.

4 See the summary by Courchene (1980).

5 See Flatters et. al. (1974) or Flatters and Purvis (1980) for example.

6 These comments are based on some current joint work with L.S. Wilson and M.B. Percy of the University of Alberta.

7 The main evidence on this is Courchene (1970).

8 Wilkinson (1980) also presents a variety of calculations based on different definitions of public sector revenue. I gratefully acknowledge his help in this section.

9 It would be appropriate to concentrate on public sector revenue alone if it were the case that the industry's share just covered cost including a normal return. I return to this below.

10 This can be seen by comparing the table on page 108 with the graph on page 112.

11 See his calculations in footnote 11.

12 The public sector share, and hence the federal share, of total revenues will rise given that the industry share includes costs incurred.

13 This assumes a price subsidy of $20.50 per barrel on an annual production of 474,500,000 barrels of oil and 284,328,000 barrels of oil-equivalent natural gas.

14 The values he presents represent the present value in end-1980 dollars rather than annual flows as in Table I.

15 See page 6, for example, where he discusses netting out import compensation payments.

16 It is interesting to note that nearly all of the waste occurs on gas in his calculations.

17 Powrie (1980, 83) makes it clear that this would apply to all provinces and all natural resources.

18 This refers to its general taxing powers and its control over interprovincial and international trade.

19 It may still play a useful role as a lower bound share. The point here is simply that events since 1973 indicated that there are no well established taxation principles that we can rely on as a guide in the event of large windfall gains.

20 Boadway and Norrie (1980) discuss the constitutional assignment over resources more fully.

BIBLIOGRAPHY

Boadway, Robin W. and Kenneth H. Norrie (1980) "Constitutional Change Canadian style: An Economic Perspective "*Canadian Public Policy* 6, No. 3 (Summer) 492-505.

Canada, Energy, Mines and Resources (1980) *The National Energy Program 1980.*

Courchene, Thomas J. (1970) "Interprovincial Migration and Economic Adjustment" *Canadian Journal of Economics* 3, No. 4 (November) 550-576.

Courchene, Thomas J. (1980) "Energy and Equalization" in Ontario Economic Council *Energy Policies for the 1980's: An Economic Analysis* Vol. 1, 103-143.

Flatters, F., J.V. Henderson, and P. Mieszkowski (1974) "Public Goods, Efficiency, and Regional Fiscal Equalization" *Journal of Public Economics* 3, 99-112.

Flatters, Frank R. and Douglas D. Purvis (1980) "Ontario: Between Alberta and the Deep Blue Sea?" Queen's University Discussion Paper No. 402.

Gainer, W.D. and T.L. Powrie (1975) "Public Revenue from Canadian Crude Petroleum Production" *Canadian Public Policy* 1, No. 1 (Winter), 1-12.

Helliwell, John F. (1980) "An Economic Evaluation of the National Energy Program" Paper presented to the Annual Conference of the Canadian Tax Foundation, Montreal, November 26.

Powrie, T.L. (1980) "Taxation and Energy" in Ontario Economic Council *op cit* Vol. 1, 73-101.

Scarfe (forthcoming) "The Federal Budget and Energy Program, October 28th, 1980: a Review" *Canadian Public Policy*.

Watkins, G.C. (1977) "Canadian Oil and Gas Pricing" in G.C. Watkins and M.A. Walker (editors) *Oil in the Seventies*, The Fraser Institute.

Watkins, G.C. (1980) "Canadian Oil Pricing" An Immaculate Deception?" Paper prepared for University of Calgary Conference "Energy: Coping in the 1980's" October 21-22.

Waverman, Leonard (1980) "The Visible Hand: The Pricing of Canadian Oil Resources" in Ontario Economic Council *op cit* Vol. 1, 25-71.

Wilkinson, B.W. (1980) "The 1980 Federal Budget, Energy Policy and All That" Paper prepared for the Canadian Tax Foundation Conference, Montreal, November 24-26.

Wilson, T.A. (1980) "Energy Policy: Overview and Macroeconomic Implications" in Ontario Economic Council *op cit* Vol. 1, 1-24.

Chapter 6

The National Energy Program and Canadian Financial Markets

DR. JOHN GRANT

Director and Chief Economist
Wood Gundy Limited,
Toronto

THE AUTHOR

JOHN A.G. GRANT was born in 1938 and received his B.A. from the University of Toronto in 1959. From 1960 to 1964 he was a Lecturer in Monetary Economics at the London School of Economics receiving his Ph.D. from that university in 1964.

Dr. Grant joined Wood Gundy Limited in 1965 and is currently Director and Chief Economist with the firm. During the period 1965 to 1970 he also served as an Assistant Professor of Economics at the University of Toronto. At Wood Gundy he heads a team of four engaged in forecasting the Canadian economy with special emphasis on the financial market. At the same time, he directs a group engaged in an intensive program of quantitative research on the behaviour of securities, prices, and yields in Canada. Dr. Grant frequently appears as a company spokesman on the outlook for markets and the economy.

The National Energy Program and Canadian Financial Markets

DR. JOHN GRANT

Director and Chief Economist
Wood Gundy Limited,
Toronto

I. INTRODUCTION

One of the major considerations in evaluating the NEP is whether it makes sense in the overall macro-economic setting. This paper argues that economic conditions will be particularly conducive to energy outlays in the next two or three years, whereas later in the 1980s there may well be significantly greater competition for scarce financial (and physical) resources. If it is thought that the NEP will tend to delay or postpone major energy outlays until mid- or late-decade, this would be a major argument against it. In particular the attitude that "the resources are in the ground and we can wait til the producers come around to our point of view" would have to be regarded as unfortunate given what we expect on the macro-economic scene in the next four years.

The paper does not take a view on whether any given project, or whether energy spending in aggregate, will be delayed or accelerated by the NEP. Nor is my intention to comment on the effect of the NEP on the financial viability of any given project. Our economic forecasting efforts at Wood Gundy have indicated, however, that Canadians' savings in the next few years are likely to grow somewhat faster than the demand for them in the economy, so financial market conditions taken overall are likely to be particularly conducive to the financing of investment in this period.

II. THE ECONOMY IN THE EARLY 1980s

The external environment

The tables and discussion that follow are largely based on Wood Gundy's forecast of the Canadian economy through 1983, dated November 1980. Our view has been and remains that a new, brief recession is about to start in the U.S., the result of collision between the Federal Reserve's monetary restraint and a persistently high inflation rate.

The Reagan Administration is committed very strongly to reducing inflationary pressures, both through "supply side" measures such as tax cuts for business, and through persistent and determined monetary restraint. In the next year or two in particular, since federal government spending will be difficult to slow, such a goal almost guarantees high interest rates relative to inflation as a tool for imposing the necessary discipline on total spending in the U.S. economy. Similar policies in Britain, Germany, France and other major countries are more or less severe according to their individual situations, but there can be little doubt that now and for some years ahead, the external environment in which Canada will have to manoeuvre will be relatively sluggish. (Major risks on world food supply and oil supply are highly important in explaining policymakers' otherwise surprising willingness to incur substantial unemployment and the associated inefficiencies — to say nothing of the political pressures.)

In the last business cycle, Canada, which had carried expansionary monetary and fiscal policies through the early stages of the world recession of 1974-75, found herself borrowing foreign capital very heavily to sustain a standard of living that was not being earned in export markets. The subsequent wage and profit controls and the marked depreciation of the Canadian dollar were unwelcome reflections of these policies, and, in fact, since 1975 the federal government and the Bank of Canada have gradually pursued a policy of restraint.

Canadian labour costs when adjusted for exchange rate effects have now become very competitive in comparison to those in our trading partner countries. However, given the very weak external environment, and the stubbornly high inflation rate, the authorities have evidently decided to continue exerting disinflationary force on the economy over the next few years.

Chart 1

Real GNP Growth, Canada vs U.S.

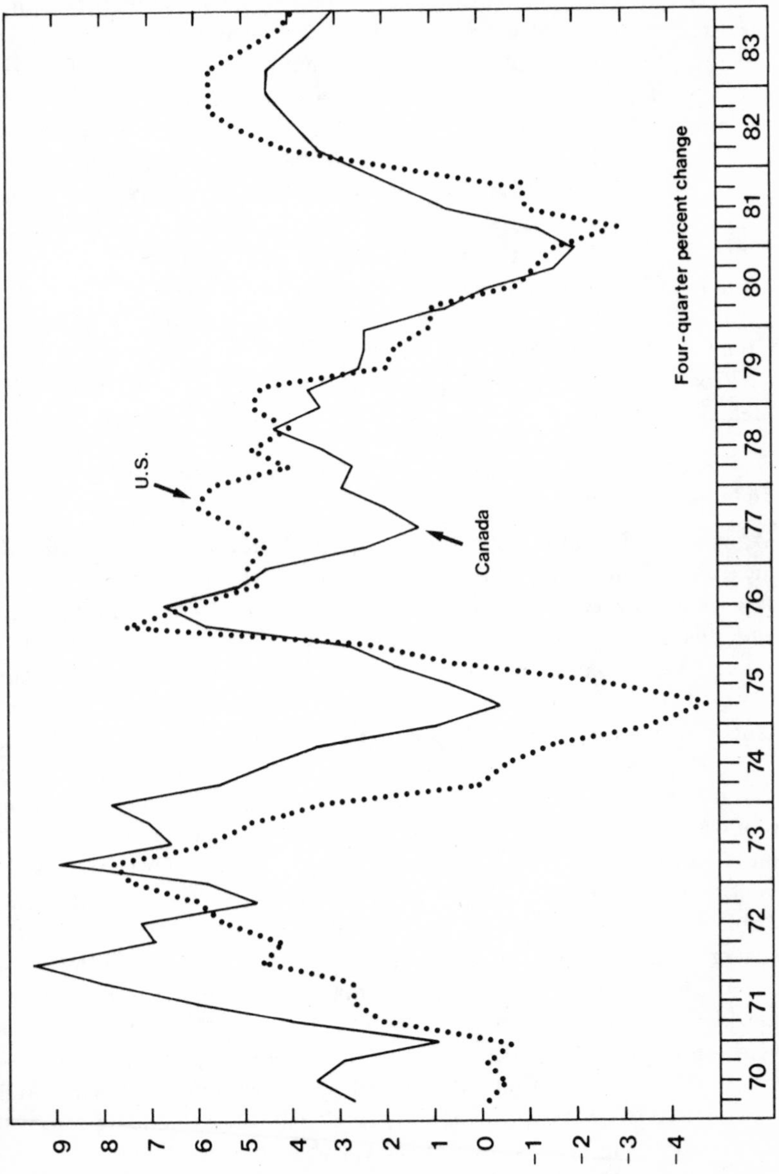

Tight fiscal policy

In fiscal policy terms this trend is intensified by the distribution of resource revenues between the two senior levels of government. The federal government is obviously not content to permit massive financial surpluses to pile up in the Western provinces while its own deficit remains high. Under the October budget and the NEP, however, the federal share of resource revenues will rise very dramatically, less at the expense of the producing provinces than at the expense of the consumers of hydrocarbons and the producing industry. Despite the promise that much of this revenue will be recycled back into Western Canada through federal participation in various projects, the overall fiscal stance of the government has become extraordinarily restrictive. Chart 2 illustrates our view of the probable trend of government deficits relative to the size of the economy, both for the federal government alone and for all three levels of government taken together.

Tight monetary policy

Monetary policy in Canada remains directed at a gradual reduction in the rate of monetary expansion. However, the economy is already experiencing very substantial underemployment of capital and labour, and this situation will probably intensify in the first half of 1981 as exports weaken and the capital stock continues to increase. We currently project that M1 growth in 1981-83 will average about 7.4 per cent a year, compared to 7.7 per cent a year in 1978-80. Despite this continued restraint, or because of it, Canada is likely to experience over-saving in the next few years. In fact, our projections of borrowing requirements related to capital spending and consumer spending are more likely to be too high than too low and, in particular the estimated major energy projects' spending levels shown in the accompanying Table I would currently be considered optimistic in the light of the struggle between Alberta and Ottawa. Moreover, as Table II indicates, one of the most important financial markets in Canada, the mortgage market, has seen a dramatic reduction in financial requirements this year, and although we do project some renewed expansion in the next few years, it is likely that with interest rates remaining relatively high mortgage borrowers will expand their demand for financing at a rate slower than the growth of funds available to meet them.

Chart 2

Government Surplus or Deficit as a Per cent of GNP

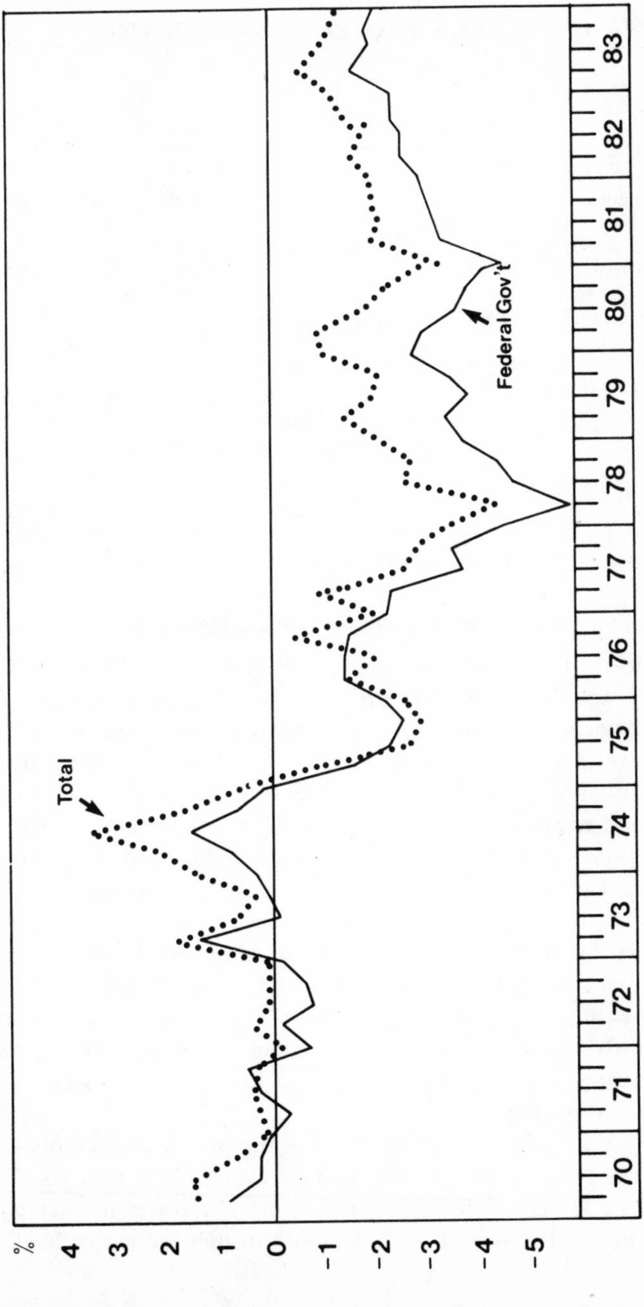

TABLE I
MAJOR ENERGY PROJECT ASSUMPTIONS
($ millions)

	1980	1981	1982	1983
Alaska Highway Gas Pipeline	250	590	550	1,870
Q and M Pipeline	70	550	480	590
Lloydminster Heavy Oil Extraction	90	100	100	100
Cold Lake Tar Sands Plant	50	100	750	1,100
Alsands Tar Sands Plant	20	50	800	1,000
SNG Plant & Benzene Plant	20	115	125	107
Great Canadian Oil Sands Plant Expansion	95	80	—	—
North-East B.C. Coal Project	—	100	300	400
Hibernia				
Grand Banks Exploration	175	200	200	200
Development	—	—	450	600
Beaufort Sea				
Exploration	200	250	250	250
Development	—	—	400	900
Hydro Quebec	2,888	2,950	3,500	3,500
Ontario Hydro	1,750	2,000	2,176	2,220

The government sector and the supply of loanable funds

Governments during the 1960s and early 1970s were a rapidly expanding sector in the economy. But since 1977, current expenditures on goods and services in this sector have not grown at all in real terms. We do project a modest expansion of real outlays, primarily at the provincial level (and especially in the West) in the next few years, but revenues from taxes and royalties will undoubtedly rise much faster than expenditure responsibilities. Of course, at the two senior levels of government, the most rapid growth in outlays in recent years has been on interest on the public debt and transfers such as unemployment insurance benefits. Even assuming continued rapid increases in these costs, my view is that, particularly at the federal level and in the Western provinces, revenue growth will dramatically outstrip expenditure growth, thus reducing the borrowing requirements of the sector as a whole and exerting a depressing effect on the demand for goods and services in the economy overall.

Table III gives a summary assessment of the pressure of supply and demand in the market for bonds issued by Canadian borrowers. The Table, like its counterpart for the mortgage market, was constructed by estimating the funds likely to be available through the major lending institutions, and similarly estimating the demand for external financing by governments, corporations and other borrowers. (A similar table was also constructed for equity financing requirements, not shown here.) In brief, Table III suggests that whereas the federal government, provincial Crown corporations and private corporations are likely to put growing pressure on the bond market as borrowers in the next few years the other major borrowing sectors are not likely to do so. Over the same period, the funds likely to be available for financing bond issues in Canada, especially from the trusteed pension funds and from the growing financial surpluses of the Western provinces, are likely to grow faster than the demand for them, which by subtraction implies that Canadians' pressures on the U.S. and European capital markets are likely to lessen, rather than grow, over the period.

Pension funds as suppliers of loanable funds

I have included in this paper Table IV illustrating our projection of the cash flows through the trusteed pension funds sector, to indicate the dramatic increases that have been taking place in this area. "Net increase in pensions" reflects primarily three sources of funds (net of pension outflows and administration costs): employee and employer contributions, and investment income (interest and dividends) from previously-acquired assets. In recent years, high rates of interest and rising corporate dividend payments have produced a dramatic increase in the cash available to the pension funds for reinvestment, and this has reinforced the continued healthy increase in wages and salaries on which contributions are based. We expect a considerable deceleration in pension funds' asset growth, but to a rapid rather than a spectacular rate. (Considerable discussion is currently taking place about possible legislative initiatives to improve the retirement income situation for Canadians who are currently not covered by pensions or who lose out on pension benefits through early job termination or for other reasons. Such legislative change will require considerable debate. When it comes, it may well lead to even *more* rapid growth of funded assets, whether in the private pension plans or in state plans. It would not appear likely that loanable funds in Canada would grow more slowly in the next few years on this account.)

TABLE II
SUPPLY AND DEMAND IN THE MORTGAGE MARKET
($ millions)

	1976A	1977A	1978A	1979A	1980F	1981F	1982F	1983F
Lenders								
Persons and Unincorporated Business	2,438	-371	3,787	3,631	4,646	4,325	4,446	5,327
Non-Financial Private Corporations	79	73	655	-70	-136	55	124	202
Government Enterprises	105	8	-15	8	8	8	8	8
Chartered Banks	1,346	2,664	3,415	2,896	842	1,870	2,859	2,714
Near Banks	5,020	6,503	6,690	8,047	5,225	6,631	8,811	9,347
Life Insurance Companies	1,024	1,454	1,089	1,571	1,060	1,463	1,920	2,035
(includes Fraternal Benefit Societies)								
Segregated Funds of Life Insurance Cos.	-	-	215	149	435	472	576	730
Trusteed Pension Funds	938	997	849	862	605	957	1,220	1,380
Other Private Financial Institutions	527	793	876	346	285	307	580	717
Public Financial Institutions								
Federal	880	624	300	27	360	325	300	300
Provincial	88	179	219	265	265	265	265	265
Federal Government	-36	-40	-52	-49	-40	-40	-40	-40
Provincial Government	455	249	-25	3	75	50	50	50
Rest of the World	68	1	60	60	27	22	47	52
Total	**12,932**	**13,134**	**18,063**	**17,746**	**13,657**	**16,710**	**21,166**	**23,088**

TABLE II (Continued)
SUPPLY AND DEMAND IN THE MORTGAGE MARKET
($ millions)

	1976A	1977A	1978A	1979A	1980F	1981F	1982F	1983F
Borrowers								
Persons and Unincorporated Business	12,048	12,472	16,829	16,798	12,538	15,484	19,982	22,225
Non-Financial Private Corporations	757	493	1,257	870	1,070	1,168	1,075	768
Government Enterprises	151	175	82	32	24	20	20	20
Near Banks	0	21	-32	8	46	40	55	42
Other Private Financial Institutions	2	1	12	9	0	7	8	9
Public Financial Institutions	25	23	-11	15	30	25	25	25
Provinces, Local Govts. and Hospitals	-51	-51	-51	-51	-51	-34	0	0
Total	**12,932**	**13,134**	**18,086**	**17,681**	**13,657**	**16,710**	**21,166**	**23,088**

Source for data through 1979: Statistics Canada, *Financial Flow Accounts*, First Quarter, 1980.

TABLE III
SUPPLY AND DEMAND IN THE BOND MARKET
($ millions)

	1976A	1977A	1978A	1979A	1980F	1981F	1982F	1983F
Purchasers								
Bank of Canada	551	1,501	627	877	800	700	600	600
Chartered Banks	588	1,065	1,213	-1,291	-1,516	500	763	710
Near Banks	255	491	837	874	1,067	527	553	605
Life Insurance Companies (includes Fraternal Benefit Societies)	1,155	1,094	1,403	1,162	2,013	2,230	2,745	2,818
Segregated Funds of Life Insurance Cos.	—	—	253	443	476	520	580	630
Trusteed Pension Funds	1,691	2,272	2,860	3,649	4,871	5,397	6,267	7,136
Other Private Financial Institutions	811	767	594	558	712	613	827	925
Public Financial Institutions (includes QPP)								
Federal	66	89	-42	-401	-100	0	0	0
Provincial	659	530	597	1,196	1,800	2,000	2,160	2,320
Provincial Governments (includes Heritage Fund)	1,642	1,813	2,169	842	2,063	4,387	4,372	5,005
Canada Pension Plan	1,519	1,654	1,674	1,914	2,022	2,027	2,068	2,067
Persons and Other Domestic Sources	134	2,420	1,996	1,870	2,189	1,580	1,468	811
Total Domestic	**9,071**	**13,696**	**14,181**	**11,693**	**16,398**	**20,481**	**22,404**	**23,627**
Rest of the World	8,627	4,922	5,257	3,703	3,500	2,800	2,600	1,800
Total	**17,698**	**18,618**	**19,438**	**15,396**	**19,898**	**23,281**	**25,004**	**25,427**
Total Marketable Bonds*	15,452	15,255	15,721	15,055	17,876	20,254	21,936	22,860
Foreign as a % of total marketable bonds	55.8	32.3	33.4	24.6	19.6	13.8	11.9	7.9

TABLE III (Continued)
SUPPLY AND DEMAND IN THE BOND MARKET
($ millions)

	1976A	1977A	1978A	1979A	1980F	1981F	1982F	1983F
Issuers								
Private Non-Financial Corporations	2,132	1,983	1,563	474	1,041	2,256	4,132	5,683
Chartered Banks	217	138	218	485	136	199	258	288
Near Banks	311	159	103	165	72	150	214	247
Other Private Financial Institutions	1,179	791	574	450	477	838	1,251	1,760
Federal Government	2,543	5,664	7,747	5,903	6,924	8,725	8,000	6,500
(of which Canada Savings Bonds)	727	1,709	2,043	-1,573	0	1,000	1,000	500
(Other)	1,816	3,955	5,704	7,476	6,924	7,725	7,000	6,000
Provinces and Hospitals	3,825	4,376	4,672	3,672	4,222	3,293	2,948	2,538
Federally-Owned Enterprises	267	97	297	130	200	520	550	250
Provincially-Owned Enterprises	5,048	3,128	2,589	2,775	4,065	4,235	4,480	4,890
Public Financial Institutions								
Federal	115	382	313	574	1,500	1,800	1,900	2,000
Provincial	282	196	223	243	250	250	250	250
Local Govts.	1,773	1,685	1,185	527	1,000	1,000	1,000	1,000
Other	6	19	-46	-2	-10	15	20	20
Total	**17,698**	**18,618**	**19,438**	**15,396**	**19,898**	**23,281**	**25,001**	**25,427**

Source for data through 1979: Statistics Canada, *Financial Flow Accounts*, First Quarter, 1980; data for years 1980 through 1983 are estimates.

*"Marketable Bonds" is defined as total issues less Canada Savings Bonds and issues sold directly to the Canada Pension Plan. It therefore includes private placements and other arrangements, not all of which may be marketable in the strict sense of the word.

TABLE IV
TRUSTEED PENSION FUNDS
($ millions)

	1976A	1977A	1978A	1979A	1980F	1981F	1982F	1983F
1. Gross Domestic Saving	0	0	0	0	0	0	0	0
2. Non-Financial Capital Acquisition	45	69	36	81	118	130	147	169
3. Net Increase in Financial Assets	3,820	4,304	5,347	6,951	8,516	9,569	11,192	13,267
Mortgages	938	997	849	862	605	957	1,220	1,380
Bonds	1,691	2,272	2,860	3,649	4,871	5,397	6,267	7,136
Shares	696	182	167	1,105	1,448	1,818	2,182	2,986
Other Assets	495	853	1,471	1,335	1,592	1,397	1,522	1,765
4. Net Increase in Pensions	3,865	4,373	5,383	7,032	8,634	9,699	11,339	13,436
5. Percent of Total Increase in Financial Assets								
Mortgages	24.6	23.2	15.9	12.4	7.1	10.0	10.9	10.4
Bonds	44.3	52.8	53.5	52.5	57.2	56.4	56.0	53.8
Shares	18.2	4.2	3.1	15.9	17.0	19.0	19.5	22.5
Other Assets	13.0	19.8	27.5	19.2	18.7	14.6	13.6	13.3

Source for data through 1979: Statistics Canada, *Financial Flow Accounts*, First Quarter, 1980; data for years 1980 through 1983 are estimates.

Alberta Heritage Savings Trust Fund

Another factor peculiar to Canada is the rapid potential increase in the surplus funds available to the Western provinces, and particularly Alberta, for investment purposes. The well-known Alberta Heritage Savings Trust Fund disposes of 30 per cent of the province's resource revenues, but the other 70 per cent will, given present prospects, increasingly itself be surplus to provincial expenditure needs. Our projections are, of course, based on the NEP as noted above. A significant renegotiation of the NEP or the federal budget which would improve the provincial revenue share or raise wellhead prices faster, would tend both to increase the province's revenues even faster and add even further to net saving flows in the economy as a whole. (Such a renegotiation might, of course, encourage greater spending by the hydrocarbons industry on exploration. But I doubt that the additional spending would surmount the levels already anticipated in our projection.)

The private demand for loanable funds

Table V, showing the sources and uses of funds of non-financial private corporations, suggests a sharp reduction during 1980 in the proportional external demand for financing by this sector compared to 1978-79. This relates to the fact that profit growth was explosive (unexpectedly so) in 1978 and 1979. Although physical investment outlays have jumped, much of the corporate cash flow has piled up in financial assets. This relatively strong "cash position" has permitted many Canadian companies to postpone long-term borrowing, despite their heavy spending. However, given major cost and spending pressures in the years ahead, we have assumed a very dramatic increase in bond (and continued heavy equity) financing in the 1981-83 period: a return, in other words, to more typical patterns, in a period of modestly profitable but not boomy expansion.

Over the decade of the 1970s and certainly up to the end of 1978, there was both a substantial acceleration in inflation and a substantial increase in the ratio of borrowings to income for every major sector in the Canadian economy. Even the personal sector, whose saving rate out of income has been close to 10 per cent for many years now and which has continued to accumulate financial assets at a rapid rate, until 1979 also permitted its liabilities to accumulate at an even more rapid rate (especially mortgage debt and consumer credit outstandings). This

TABLE V
NON-FINANCIAL PRIVATE CORPORATIONS
($ millions)

	1976A	1977A	1978A	1979A	1980F	1981F	1982F	1983F
1. **Gross Domestic Saving**	16,802	16,954	18,664	24,176	25,797	28,402	32,865	36,711
Capital Consumption Allowance	10,638	11,711	12,681	13,871	14,937	17,336	19,782	22,428
Net Domestic Saving	6,164	5,243	5,983	10,305	10,860	11,066	13,083	14,283
2. **Non-Financial Capital Acquisition**	20,605	21,712	23,518	31,457	35,451	37,538	44,460	50,978
Gross Fixed Capital Formation	20,138	21,803	23,660	27,634	32,107	35,951	41,447	47,826
Change in Phys. Value of Inventories & Purchase of Existing Assets	467	-91	-142	3,823	3,344	1,587	2,960	3,152
3. **Net Increase in Financial Assets**	5,610	8,729	17,879	19,247	12,668	13,884	15,120	16,453
Receivables	2,238	3,794	8,192	7,057	5,093	5,553	6,411	7,138
Loans	-130	480	556	341	228	305	438	527
Claims on Associated Enterprises	1,452	2,926	3,768	6,935	5,390	5,956	6,548	7,324
Other Assets	2,050	1,529	5,363	4,914	1,958	2,068	1,723	1,464
4. **Net Financing Requirement** (3 + 2 – 1 + discrepancy)	10,819	12,576	23,378	28,068	22,323	23,019	26,661	30,720

TABLE V (Continued)
NON-FINANCIAL PRIVATE CORPORATIONS
($ millions)

	1976A	1977A	1978A	1979A	1980F	1981F	1982F	1983F
5. **Financed by:**								
Payables	1,177	1,960	5,701	6,420	3,788	4,535	5,092	5,499
Loans	3,690	2,064	4,826	7,345	6,914	5,755	6,399	7,373
Short-Term Paper	353	-409	477	994	434	552	533	614
Claims on Associated Enterprises	1,103	1,927	1,466	2,026	2,603	2,434	2,300	2,212
Mortgages	757	493	1,257	870	1,070	1,168	1,075	768
Bonds (net)	2,132	1,983	1,563	474	1,041	2,256	4,132	5,683
Share Capital	927	2,675	4,782	5,260	5,514	5,686	6,132	7,619
Other	680	1,883	3,306	4,679	958	634	998	952
6. **Discrepancy**	1,406	-911	645	1,540	0	0	0	0
7. **Gross New Bond Issues**	3,060	3,900	2,005	1,937	2,037	3,318	5,366	7,785
Retirements (Maturities, Sinking Funds, etc)	928	1,917	442	1,463	996	1,062	1,234	2,102

Source for data through 1979: Statistics Canada, *Financial Flow Accounts*, First Quarter, 1980; data for years 1980 through 1983 are estimates.

cumulative process has gradually increased the burden on consumers of servicing this debt, a burden which has recently grown particularly rapidly as interest rates finally rose faster than inflation.

Recently, we have seen what may be the beginning of a long-run trend to reduce borrowings relative to income. The sharp drop in mortgage borrowing this year, the reduction in the growth of consumer credit, the virtual cessation of corporate fixed-interest borrowing at long term, and the evident efforts noted above by all levels of government to raise revenues faster than expenditures suggest that either monetary restraint is "working" or that all sectors are prudently moving to protect their solvency in the event of a prolonged deflationary experience. Fortunately, in the last two years corporate profitability has grown very dramatically, and this, coupled with the effective reduction in the ratio of corporate debt to total equity employed, has created a "virtuous circle" whereby investors have driven up share prices, thus encouraging even more rapid increase in equity financing and a further strengthening of corporate balance sheets. (The growing challenge, then, for corporations will be to earn a high return on this equity, for despite its being *relatively* cheap compared to earlier periods, equity remains the most expensive (although most flexible) form of financing.)

Now if all sectors, governments, corporations *and* individuals are trying to reduce their interest burdens, then in large measure they must be doing so by diverting income into debt repayment rather than into fresh purchases of goods and services. In other words, a downward multiplier has taken hold. (Canadians have been reasonably effective in passing forward these pressures to foreign countries as well: between the third quarters of 1979 and 1980, real ($71) imports are estimated to have dropped by some $3.2 billion, or 8.7 per cent.) In the early stage of this episode, therefore, a primary impetus in all three sectors is to reduce the ratio of indebtedness to income. As long as the real interest rate remains relatively high, it will remain prudent to do so.

III. THE NATIONAL ENERGY PROGRAM IN FINANCIAL PERSPECTIVE

The picture I have been painting is therefore one in which, far from placing heavy strain on Canada's financial capacity, the projected development of Western energy resources will be a very welcome addition to domestic uses of funds, at least in the next few years. Projection into the mid- and late-1980s is not so easy. However, some general statements can probably be essayed.

First, the general question of macro-economic policy. There can as yet be no real confidence among senior policy advisors of world governments that the productivity losses associated with rapid energy price escalation are going to moderate. The more there is incentive to develop expensive hydrocarbon sources, the more likely it is that most world economies will be struggling precariously to simply maintain overall living standards, far from seeing them improve. In many countries of the world, the arithmetic of population increase suggests a continuing, deep crisis as the next two decades proceed, adding to the world's instability and making more difficult the expansion of world trade.

Monetary policy has in the last few years borne the brunt of efforts to reduce economic growth to what can be afforded. Fiscal policy, as mentioned above, is slowly but generally becoming less generous as well, as governments around the world try to free scarce resources for private investment, at the expense of the scaffolding of income-transfer and consumption-supporting programs funded by government deficits that have mounted in most countries in response to inflation and recession. It would appear likely in the next few years that fiscal policies will generally continue to "tighten", even though monetary policies may once again "loosen", the degree of loosening being severely constrained by the degree of progress made in restoring productivity growth.

Canada, in principle, is one of the nations *least* constrained by considerations of prudence from returning to stimulative policies, because as a high-saving country with a falling dependency ratio, it can easily divert resources into investment without having to restrain consumption decisions or the level of government services so severely as most other countries. The appropriate degree of monetary tightness will be chosen to reflect a political judgement about the appropriate trade-off between slack and progress against inflation. We may well be in a position by the mid-1980s of wanting to get on with a major program of investment in a multitude of industries, many of them export-related. By that time, inflationary pressures may have subsided considerably in North America, with living standards growing essentially at a rate consistent with our productivity.

The critical issue of timing

If the NEP has the effect of weakening private investment outlays in the early years, followed by a positive effect in the mid- to late-1980s (e.g. if the program is revised significantly in such a way as to encourage a substantially higher, but later, level of energy development spending) then we may face a renewed "bunching" problem after all. The discussion so far in this paper has suggested that there is likely to be ample "room" in the Canadian financial markets in the next few years (and probably in 1984) to meet the financial requirements of the proposed major energy projects and a heavy program of non-energy private investment outlays as well. If these are delayed, however, then we face two sorts of questions: what will fill the macro-financing "gap" in 1982 and 1983? and, when the major projects do get underway, will they tend to give rise to a "boom" situation in the mid-1980s which will require major macro-policy initiatives to prevent a return to the inflationary conditions of the 1970s? We should recognize the degree to which the debt-reduction efforts of the current period reflect tight monetary restraint and a historically over-borrowed position in most sectors. Once consumers and businessmen and governments have reduced their debt burdens to more sensible levels, the urge to expand will once again come to the fore.

Although much public commentary has focused on the realism or lack of it in the NEP with respect to its impact on the country's self-sufficiency in hydrocarbons, this paper suggests that we should recognize the relatively favourable conditions likely to prevail in Canadian financial markets in the early years of the decade, and note the potential problems of macro-economic management entailed if there are major postponements to mid-decade or later. It would be most unfortunate if we would once again have to crank up monetary and fiscal restraints in *that* time period, having just lived through the pain they create. It would be particularly undesirable if the reason for renewed restraint turned out to be a "bunching" of energy and non-energy investment projects.